A Handbook for
the Study of Drama

By the same authors:

A HANDBOOK FOR THE STUDY OF FICTION
A HANDBOOK FOR THE STUDY OF POETRY

A
HANDBOOK FOR
THE STUDY OF DRAMA

by

LYNN ALTENBERND
University of Illinois

and

LESLIE L. LEWIS
University of Colorado

The Macmillan Company, New York
Collier-Macmillan Limited, London

ACKNOWLEDGMENT

Act I from *The Second Mrs. Tanqueray* by Sir Arthur Wing Pinero is reprinted by permission of the Directors of Samuel French Ltd., Trustees for the Estate of the late Sir Arthur Wing Pinero.

Fourth Printing, 1970

This book is a revised and expanded version of part one of *Introduction to Literature: Plays* by Lynn Altenbernd and Leslie L. Lewis, © copyright 1963 by The Macmillan Company.

Library of Congress catalog card number: 66–14196

THE MACMILLAN COMPANY
866 THIRD AVENUE, NEW YORK, NEW YORK 10022
Collier-Macmillan Canada, Ltd., Toronto, Ontario

Printed in the United States of America

Introduction

The three little books called A *Handbook for the Study of Fiction*, A *Handbook for the Study of Poetry*, and A *Handbook for the Study of Drama* are revisions and enlargements of the handbook sections in our *Introduction to Literature: Stories, Poems, Plays*. In their present form the handbooks are intended for use with editions of individual works or with any anthology that lacks similar instructional materials. These books are intended to facilitate rather than to forestall classroom discussion—hence, they set forth their principles briefly, without elaboration, and with modest amounts of illustration. The authors have concentrated on preliminary and elementary suggestions for reading literary works. Thus the student with little earlier experience in these matters may find help in getting started, whereas the more advanced student should find the handbooks useful for review. Often the teacher may wish to develop points beyond our discussion of them or, if the class procedure is inductive, to use the handbooks as references that succinctly summarize the discussion. Of course, they are no substitute for the guidance of an intelligent and sympathetic teacher.

A *Handbook for the Study of Drama* covers the nature and elements of drama, traditional types of plays, and the nature of modern plays, and tries to indicate the connection between theaters and societies. Also, it concentrates on overcoming the initial difficulties in reading plays, particularly on absorbing the exposition and reading the play as drama.

Urbana, Illinois	L. A.
Boulder, Colorado	L. L. L.

Contents

I. THE NATURE OF DRAMA   1

II. THE DRAMA AS LITERATURE   5

III. THE ELEMENTS OF DRAMA   11

     A. Dramatic Conventions   11
     B. The Play Story   12
     C. Characters   13
     D. Plot   16

IV. DIALOGUE AND ACTION   25

V. READING THE FIRST ACT   33

VI. MEANING IN DRAMA   61

VII. TRADITIONAL TYPES OF PLAYS   65

     A. Farce   67
     B. Comedy   68
     C. Melodrama, Drame, and Problem Play   69
     D. Tragedy   70

VIII. MODERN PLAYS   75

For Further Reading   79

Index   83

Contents

A Handbook for
the Study of Drama

I

The Nature of Drama

Drama is a narrative art, one of several modes in which mankind has learned to present a story. Stories are presented to give pleasure, to entertain. In addition, they have a wide range of functions in a society; they may, for example, conserve its legends, order its laws, explore its problems, demonstrate its codes, ridicule its weaknesses, or extend its knowledge. Stories must in some way happen within the range of human nature; the emotions of the characters, their reasons for doing as they do, and how it feels to them to be in such situations must be within the range of responses of the recipient of the story. If the story is of an age and order of ideas different from his own, he must be able to transplant himself—to be an ancient Greek, a medieval man, a renaissance man. Stories may be heard as recited by a storyteller, read by a solitary reader, or seen and heard in the dramatic mode by a spectator in a theater. Our concern here is with a fourth mode of enjoying a story—that of the reader of a play.

Drama is composed not for a reader, as fiction and poetry are, but for spectators. The playright composes under a knowledge of the limitations and advantages of a specific kind of theater. He then entrusts his play to a director and actors, who produce the play before an audience. The production is interpreted and executed for a given kind of stage in a given kind of theater, the particular kind varying in different periods. The audience reacts as a group, interprets, and varies in its interpretations not only from age to age but from night to night, from matinee to evening. What the playwright sets down in words is usually restricted to directions for the setting and costuming, directions for the acting, and the speeches of the characters. The result is "an imitation of an action," a story acted by its characters. In ideal completeness, the result comes to a spectator who as one in an audience sees, hears, and feels the total effect of the performed play in the "dramatic present."

The dramatic present is a complex spell cast over the spectators as they unite in *seeing* and *hearing* a story which is happening *there*, on the stage before them. Playwrights are at one with actors, directors, and technicians in dedication to living performances, with each performance, ideally, happening for the first time, and with no one aware of the conclusion until the conclusion appears. Reflection and criticism must wait until the final curtain; immediacy and intensity are re-created in each performance before each audience. Even though the spectator is aware that he is in a theater, watching a performance, and that he knows the outcome of the play, the pull of the dramatic present is forward.

The amount of story presented is foreshortened in a play; the action is initiated as close as possible to its final issue. The incidents are of high tension to start with, and the tension increases rapidly. The sense of finality, of hurrying to a conclusion, increases with each of the few incidents which can be exhibited in the limited time for a performance. The characters, under the pressure of the action, make discoveries and decisions rapidly. The pace and intensity of drama give it its characteristic "dramatic" effect, an effect calculated for projection through an audience.

According to Aristotle, the playwright is combining six

elements in a play: action, character, thought, language, music, and spectacle. Plays are not miscellaneous, episodic, or accidental, but artfully calculated and wrought, each one unified and made probable under its own assumptions and totality. Unity and probability, the pervasive qualities of plays, are produced within each play by careful harmonizing of the dramatic elements. A play is, in the best sense of the word, artificial, the work of an artificer, and of an artificer working with many arts and many nonverbal resources.

II

The Drama as Literature

With a theater, a stage, actors, an audience, and resources of music and spectacle, dance, and pantomime, gesture, action, costume, setting, and histrionics to draw on in the creation of a unified and probable play, the playwright is obviously composing a work of art with more than words. The playwright, however, uses words, and his product is thus a form of literature. A play exists on paper, before and after its performance; hence it can be read. Like fiction, it tells a story; like poetry, it makes imaginative use of language. Shakespeare's plays were first printed in 1623; his readers have subsequently far outnumbered his spectators.

It is a paradoxical tribute to the power and permanence of great plays that they will have a reading audience long after, and far distant from, the specific theatrical conditions under which they were first produced—just as they will be produced under theatrical conditions far different from those for which they were composed. Aristotle in the *Poetics* analyzed, partly on the basis of reading, the tragedies of Aeschylus, Sophocles, and Euripides, which had been composed and produced more than a half century before. The tragedies he analyzed were composed for performance in an outdoor amphitheater, but they have subsequently been produced indoors on proscenium stages.

Similarly, Shakespeare's plays have been read by people who have never seen them performed, and have been performed in outdoor theaters resembling the Greek and in indoor theaters resembling everything from a barn to an opera house, although the nature of the Elizabethan stage was a factor in Shakespeare's composition.

Editors now supply the reader of early plays with helpful initial information which compensates for the bareness of the original text. Increasingly in modern times the playwright knows that if his play makes a genuine impact in the theater, it will be read by a great number of people who follow the drama as readers whether they can be spectators or not. Playwrights have even become somewhat merciful to, or considerate of, the reader in supplying more external guidance to the time, place, setting, and characters. With a touch of the whimsical essayist in his nature, J. M. Barrie first broke the rule of subtracting the playwright from the play in his published versions by inserting in his stage directions comments which were not expected to be directions to his actors. In *What Every Woman Knows* he remarks that there is nothing more comfortable than a horsehair chair if it has a good slit down the middle, and that Maggie, who is not good-looking, enters with her throat cut, so to speak, from ear to ear. George Bernard Shaw expanded both the descriptive and interpretive support of the dialogue in the versions of his plays published to be read. His prefaces, often added to after the play had been performed, draw the reader's attention to values in the play and to the significance of such values in society and life.

More important to the reader of a play than such postmortem discussion are the expanded descriptions of scenes and characters in modern published plays. The playwright here has an opportunity to reach the reader with clues to the interpretation he hopes for, in the knowledge that his play, in this version, is to be read by a solitary spectator, who needs assistance in endowing the action with its full dramatic effect.

The solitary spectator poring over the text of a play is certainly not in the same relation to the play that he would be in if he were one of an audience watching a performance. Neither, however, is he quite in the position of the reader of a novel or of a poem. A play heavily equipped with interpretative prefaces (even by Shaw) is, as a novel, a bad novel. It is true that there is a kind of novel reader who tries to skip all the text except the dialogue, and a kind of novelist who tries to write the so-called dramatic novel—one which reduces the text as far as possible to dialogue. The novelist, however, is still composing for his art form, one which permits extension, omniscience, authorial intrusion, and many other devices forbidden to the playwright by the nature of the dramatic mode. The novelist may do all the work for the reader, even to telling him what he has read. The dramatist may do something for the reader by his title, informative stage directions, and descriptive cast of characters. The rest is dialogue, out of which the solitary spectator must make his play himself.

Whether the play reader should stage the play in his imagination as he reads it, to overcome the disadvantage of being at home rather than at the theater, or take advantage of his opportunity to read it as he reads a novel, is a question for which there is no dogmatic answer. The entire force of the playwright's art has been directed toward making the reader perform the play on a stage— even, if the reader is well-enough informed, on the particular kind of stage for which the playwright composed it: the open-air arena for Sophocles, the unlocalized and fluid Elizabethan stage for Shakespeare, the room with one wall removed for Ibsen. However, the stage to any playwright is a physical facility upon which he calculates how to reveal a story. The story will owe its vitality, finally, to our ability to relate it to life. The reader may therefore read through the stage to reality or directly from the page to reality. In reading *Romeo and Juliet* he may re-create "fair Verona, where we lay our scene," as a town in medieval Italy, as the stage of the Globe Theatre in Shakespeare's London, or as some ideal stage of his own designing. Whether he identifies himself with the protagonist or the director, whether he reads *to* the stage, *through* the stage, or *without* the stage, he is invited even by the printed play to yield to the unfolding situation, to see and hear, to form an active imaginative equivalent to the play. A more complete appreciation of the playwright's skill in overcoming the difficulties of the complex dramatic medium may come only with a second reading; certainly the perception of the artistry of a playwright is a rich addition to the first natural apprehension of a play.

Offering the play reader any alternative to "staging" the play as he reads involves an element of treason to the dedication of the play to the stage by playwright, director, and cast. By way of amends, the editors add their belief that the play reader, starting with that degree of familiarity with the dramatic process he has gained from seeing plays and films and from reading poetry and fiction, will find a double enrichment in seeing plays produced as often as he can. His experiences as a reader will make him a more receptive and sensitive theatergoer; and his theater experience will make him a fuller reader. We do not really agree with George Jean Nathan, that inveterate playgoer, when he said (in an introduction to an anthology, of course), "Plays are meant to be acted well; if they are not thus well acted it is better that they be read than seen." We believe it is better to read a good play than neither to see it nor read it; we also believe that reading a play either before or after seeing it performed on stage or screen is a source of pleasure and understanding equal to that provided by reading fiction and poetry. Drama makes powerful comments on human nature and the human condition; it reveals human truth arising out of characters under the pressure of situation; it is a persuasive and memorable mode of conveying truth. Every civilized society has provided itself with the means of projecting itself, testing itself, exploring and judging itself in its theater.

III

The Elements of Drama

A. Dramatic Conventions

A play is manifestly not a real but an artificial representation of life. It asks from the audience an active adoption of the rules of the game—an acceptance of a good many dramatic conventions, in the spirit of "willing suspension of disbelief." Spectators know that they are in a theater; they bought tickets and found their seats. They know that the scene is only a scene on a stage; they saw the curtain drawn to reveal it. Within the play itself they accept conventions of time and space: a presentation of scenes years apart compressed into two hours, events most unnaturally uninterrupted by accidental distractions, and speech dealing unnaturally with one subject. They accept arrested time while they walk about between acts. They accept as whispers speeches loud enough to be heard in the balcony, asides heard by them and not by characters on the stage a few feet away from the speaker, soliloquies in which a character tells them more of himself than his fellow characters know, and so on ad infinitum. Some conventions are inherent in all drama; some are "dated" to conditions and modes in particular times. All conventions are a testimony to the pleasure the audience expects to receive by adopting them. The reader of a play should similarly

adopt them, insofar as the printed play calls for their adop
tion, as concessions made to have an imaginatively or
dramatically true experience of a play. Within the play
unity and probability are built upon the dramatic conven
tions.

B. The Play Story

A play compels "willing suspension of disbelief" for the
artificial nature of the dramatic mode by offering a *story*
that is clear, strong, and progressive enough to be placed
or met within the dramatic world. The story base of a
play may be original with the dramatist or borrowed from
legend, history, or fiction. Greek and Elizabethan dra
matists commonly took a story already well known. The
Joan of Arc story has been used by Shaw in *Saint Joan* and
by Anouilh in *The Lark*. Oedipus of Thebes, Richard II,
Mary, Queen of Scots, and Antigone, among others, have
had more than one play constructed from their stories.
Lorca is said to have developed *Blood Wedding* from a
newspaper clipping he had kept for years.

Many stories are the original invention of the playwright. He may draw on his own life experiences, his
memories, his reactions to the kind of life led by the people
in places he has known. He may invent the story to express
the characters or to protest against their environment. His
initial impulse may come from an interest in situation,
character, or theme.

Nowadays a short story or novel may become the basis
of a play; an original play story or a novel or a short story
may become the basis of a motion picture; any or all of
them may become the basis of a television play. A good
story, one into which perceptive interpretation of human
life has been packed, will give pleasure in all four forms.

A natural but superficial complaint of the reader of a
novel who subsequently sees it in play or screenplay form
is that it has been changed. The dramatist left out a char-

:ter; he suppressed a subplot; he changed the *reasons* for ιe actions of the characters. To note *why* the dramatist ιade the changes—how the total of the changes accounts ɔr a good play made from a good novel or a good screen-lay from a good play—is an illuminating exercise, but it ιould start from a recognition that changes *will be made* ι any story as it is handled in a different medium. The ramatist may change many elements in a novel: the num-er and order of incidents, the number and the motives f characters, the atmosphere of the scenes, even, some-mes, the theme. More than one play is thus possible from single life or a single story, more than one screenplay ɔm a single play. Each has required an artist concentrated ɩ making an intensely particular use of the source story ·ithin his mode.

What the playwright sees in a story, from whatever ɔurce, is a chance to develop it in a particular way to reate the effect and express the meaning he has decided it an be made to have in his play. As playwright he has been alled an artificer, joiner, chess player, architect—all terms alling attention to the necessity of careful workmanship ɔ get a story constructed for the stage. Henry James has ιid. "The fine thing in a real drama, generally speaking, is hat more than any other work of literary art, it needs a ιasterly structure. It needs to be shaped and fashioned nd laid together, and this process makes a demand upon n artist's rarest gifts. He must combine and arrange, in-erpolate and eliminate, play the joiner with the most ttentive skill; and yet at the end effectually bury his tools nd his sawdust, and invest his elaborate skeleton with the moothest and most polished integument."

⊃. Characters

That the basis of a play (the unifying center to which he other dramatic elements contribute) is its action, the hing done, is a rule that supplies the reader his best connection with most plays. From Aristotle, again: "The plot being an imitation of an action, must imitate one action and that a whole, the structural union of the parts being such that, if any one of them is displaced or removed, the whole will be disjointed and disturbed." However, a good play does not give the impression that it is a plot being acted out but that it is a group of characters acting as they must. The emotions of the characters give interest to the plot; the story seems to be what it has to be because the characters are as they are. The sense of probability (that these things could have happened under the conditions revealed by the play) and the sense of necessity (that they had to happen as they did) are alike served by the intimate or organic fusion of characters and action. As Brander Matthews said, "The conjunction of character and action is no chance mechanical mixture; it is rather an intimate chemical union." To put this another way: that some critics hold emotion rather than action to be the true stuff of drama is a tribute to the fusion of character and plot achieved by the playwright. The plot governs, but imperceptibly, because its development is conceived as necessary for its particular agents. We shall therefore touch on characters in drama and then turn to plot.

The cast of characters in a play will usually be as small as the dramatist can manage for unfolding his story. Having only two or three hours for the play, and needing to develop and exhibit the *essentials* of the situation fully, he will restrict himself not only in time (starting late in the story) but in characters. Some time must go to establishing any character; if the interest is dispersed it is being substracted from the principals and dissipating the impressions. Just as the action of a play is compressed, characters are suppressed, so that each character included in a play is used to carry his share of the action and to carry his full typical weight in the representative world of the play.

Not all of the characters even in a selective cast will achieve an equal distinctness and individuality. Because the action must move as fast as characterization will let it, or impel it, the action must center on a few principal characters. No formula for major and minor characters holds for all plays, but the play reader will find it helpful to distinguish as quickly as possible between major, individualized characters and minor, more typical characters. It is not a reproach to a playwright to note that some of his characters are quickly established types—the play is not about them, and the time saved in characterizing them briefly by establishing the type pattern can be spent on the major characters and the major action.

Some modern playwrights, William Saroyan and William Inge, for example, do try to distribute the interest over a larger number of characters, which also means they try to distribute the action or the theme over a larger number, but there are still some type characters. Older dramatists worked in a social and intellectual milieu that was proud of its skill in assigning typical traits to many of the members of the society; Molière and Shakespeare drew freely upon the types their own age and society had identified and created characteristic behavior for: the pedant, the fop, the braggart, the soldier, the hypocrite, the gallant.

The main character in a plot—the one the dramatic pressure centers upon—is called the *protagonist*; his opponent is called the *antagonist*, or if not a person, the *antagonistic force*. Other roles which recur in drama because their functions are inherent in the nature of plot are the *confidant* (feminine *confidante*), in whom a major character confides; and the *foil*, who contrasts with, or is the opposite of, the protagonist.

The dramatic mode tends to isolate the characters in a play from all interpretation of themselves except that which they give to one another in the play situation of which they are a part. To create a sense of what they were like before the play began and will be like after it has ended calls for a reach and insight on the dramatist's part to realize them, and a rich manipulation of language and action to project them. Many ephemeral plays contain characters who merely act the part the plot calls for and we forget them with the fall of the curtain. Characters who so complete themselves that they are remembered as persons outside the details of their stories, as the creators rather than the victims of the dramatic necessity they served, give permanence to the play: Hamlet, Oedipus, Caliban, Shylock, Antigone, Hedda Gabler, Cyrano, Lear, Joan of Arc.

The playwright has several ways in which to characterize. He has, first of all, the appearance of the character, which he often specifies in the stage directions. The age, sex, size, dress, and general physical type are instantly visible, probably more effectively so on the stage than in the descriptive characterizations of fiction. Each character appears "made-up" for his part. The type or mold is quickly established. He then starts talking and acting. He may talk to the audience in asides and soliloquies or to another character about a third. Language is an intimate characteristic —not only what a character says but how he says it. In the interplay of characters, what each says about the others becomes indirect characterization of himself and of his subject. As the characters in a play proceed from talking about themselves and the other characters to talking in the action of the play, and taking positions in relation to that action, the interdependence of action and character becomes characterizing in itself. What kind of person would decide to do this for that reason? Attraction, repulsion, or objectivity toward the characters is created by what they seem to be, what they seem to be doing, and why.

D. Plot

The playwright orders and connects the events in a story to form a plot, a causal or motivated sequence of actions which introduce a conflict into the lives of a group of characters, cause them to decide on certain courses of conduct in relation to the change, follow the alternating efforts of the two sides to a conclusion, and give a glimpse of the new state of affairs which arises as a result of the struggle.

That conflict is the basis of plot is another "rule rather than exception" in dramatic theory; many more plays have conflict plots than not. Most plays initiate a "purposive will," or free choice, of a course of action by the challenged character; it is the pursuit of this purpose to its conclusion which gives coherence to the plot. The kind of person he is, and the kind of persons he is engaged with and against in a conflict, thus become a condition of the plot at the time of its inception, and characters, the agents of the plot, often seem to be what the play is about.

In analyzing a plot, we will give most of our space not to its general nature, which is already familiar, but to the methods forced upon the playwright by the nature of the dramatic form. The common parts of a plot are:

1. The exposition, or preliminary situation.
2. The inciting or exciting force, or challenge.
3. The rising action, or complication.
4. The climax, or turning point (sometimes preceded by the crisis, which makes the direction of the turn final).
5. The denouement, resolution, or (in tragedy) catastrophe.

1. *Exposition and Inciting Force*

The *exposition* is all the information necessary for the reader to grasp the initial situation, to be able to go on with the play. A novelist may supply a "long foreground," a section of plain narrative dealing in a leisurely way with the preliminary situation, full of characterizing incidents that familiarize the reader with the potentials of the various characters before pressure is put upon them by the complication. The dramatist has no time for this; the time of a play is limited; the plot and not the preconditions of the plot is the heart of the matter. The members of the audience want to see and hear the situation develop as fast as their information allows them to grasp it. There was a time, in Thebes, when Antigone's brother had not been denied burial; a time in Venice when Brabantio's daughter Desdemona had not married Othello, the Moor; a time in Verona when (presumably) the Capulets and Montagues were not feuding, and certainly before Romeo, a Montague, and Juliet, a Capulet, fell in love. *Antigone*, however, opens after the death of Polynices, with Antigone already confronted with the edict of Creon against burying her dead brother; *Othello* opens with Iago and Roderigo arousing Brabantio to rescue his daughter from the Moor; *Romeo and Juliet* opens (following the Prologue) with a street brawl between Capulets and Montagues, after which the fiery Tybalt, a Capulet, recognizes Romeo as a Montague. The reader is hard-pressed to get things sorted out, the people placed. He scents a future conflict between Antigone and Creon, between Iago and Othello, and between Romeo and Tybalt. He is carried forward, is then delayed for further exposition, is then carried forward again.

Yet from the outset the exposition must be clear; who are these people, where are they, when is it, who is speaking to whom about what? The first revelations about the characters are also a matter of exposition. They must be "placed" by the reader before he can respond to the complication. The playwright, in developing exposition in a forward-moving situation, extends knowledge of the preliminary situation backward, and rounds out characters gradually by material that extends their pasts, reveals their secrets, or multiplies examples of their reactions. The presence of the past in the present or the pressure of a plot situation to force out of the characters secrets from their past lives is particularly suited to the dramatic mode. Ibsen, specially, often begins very late in the situation and makes disclosures of the difference between the initial glimpse of the character and the final truth both expository and dramatic.

The play reader as compared with the spectator is at no time at a greater disadvantage than at the drawing of the curtain at the opening of the play. On the stage the spectator can *see* the place, *see and hear* the characters, quickly sort them out, size them up, and move forward with the unfolding situation. Because we believe that the taking hold of a play by the reader at the outset is the key to his catching up with the spectator, we shall devote much of our brief space for play structure to the exposition and common devices for establishing it, and shall end this section with a first act as an illustration of expository practices in drama.

The first aids offered by the playwright are the printed preliminaries. The title of the play, the time and place of the action, the setting, and the cast of characters—as much preconditioning of the imagination as possible—are usually given before the first scene. The reader will do well to start slowly, assimilating in advance what to expect. Prologues were often used for this preliminary conditioning in earlier plays, as in *Romeo and Juliet*.

> Two households, both alike in dignity,
> In fair Verona, where we lay our scene,
> From ancient grudge break to new mutiny,
> Where civil blood makes civil hands unclean.
> From forth the fatal loins of these two foes
> A pair of star-cross'd lovers take their life;
> Whose misadventur'd piteous overthrows
> Doth with their death bury their parents' strife.
> The fearful passage of their death-mark'd love,
> And the continuance of their parents' rage,
> Which, but their children's end, nought could remove,
> Is now the two hours' traffic of our stage;

The which if you with patient care attend,
What here shall miss, our toil shall strive to mend.

Having a large and loose action to handle in *Henry V*
Shakespeare invites his audience both to comprehend tha
the play deals with warlike Harry's invasion of France an
victory at Agincourt and to "swell the scene."

O for a Muse of fire, that would ascend
The brightest heaven of invention,
A kingdom for a stage, princes to act,
And monarchs to behold the swelling scene!
Then should the warlike Harry, like himself,
Assume the port of Mars; and at his heels,
Leash'd in like hounds, should famine, sword, and fire
Crouch for employment. But pardon, gentles all,
The flat unraised spirits that have dar'd
On this unworthy scaffold to bring forth
So great an object. Can this cockpit hold
The vasty fields of France? or may we cram
Within this wooden O the very casques
That did affright the air at Agincourt? . . .

In Act III, having a scene shift in mid-act, the Prologue
serves again:

But, till the King come forth, and not till then
Unto Southampton do we shift our scene.

The Prologue may furnish a clue to the unifying idea of a
play, as well as to its initial situation, as "scandal" is the
Prologue's subject in Sheridan's *The School for Scandal*,
preceding an opening scene in which Lady Sneerwell is
conferring with Snake on the ruining of reputations in
general and of Charles Surface's reputation in particular.
Two servants talking about their masters, a time-honored
device now out of fashion but still charmingly clear and
direct, took care of the opening of many fine old plays.
They did not *complete* the exposition, but they initiated it
with some arousing of expectation, as in Sheridan's *The
Rivals*.

SCENE: *A street in Bath.*

(COACHMAN *crosses the stage.—Enter* FAG, *looking after him.*)

FAG. What! — Thomas! — Sure, 'tis he? — What! — Thomas!—Thomas!

COACHMAN. Hey!—Odd's life!—Mr. Fag!—give us your hand, my old fellow-servant.

FAG. Excuse my glove, Thomas:—I'm dev'lish glad to see you, my lad: why, my prince of charioteers, you look as hearty!—but who the deuce thought of seeing you in Bath!

COACHMAN. Sure, Master, Madam Julia, Harry, Mrs. Kate, and the postilion be all come!

FAG. Indeed!

COACHMAN. Aye! Master thought another fit of the gout was coming to make him a visit: so he'd a mind to gi't the slip, and whip! we were all off at an hour's warning.

FAG. Aye, aye! hasty in everything, or it would not be Sir Anthony Absolute!

COACHMAN. But tell us, Mr. Fag, how does young master? Odd! Sir Anthony will stare to see the Captain here!

FAG. I do not serve Captain Absolute now.

COACHMAN. Why sure!

FAG. At present I am employed by Ensign Beverley.

COACHMAN. I doubt, Mr. Fag, you ha'n't changed for the better.

FAG. I have not changed Thomas.

COACHMAN. No! why, didn't you say you had left young master?

FAG. No.——Well, honest Thomas, I must puzzle you no farther: briefly then—Captain Absolute and Ensign Beverley are one and the same person.

COACHMAN. The devil they are!

FAG. So it is indeed, Thomas; and the *Ensign*-half of my master being on guard at present—the *Captain* has nothing to do with me.

COACHMAN. So, so!—What, this is some freak, I warrant!——Do tell us, Mr. Fag, the meaning o't—you know I ha' trusted you.

FAG. You'll be secret, Thomas?

COACHMAN. As a coach-horse.

FAG. Why then the cause of all this is—LOVE—Love, Thomas, who (as you may get read to you) has been a masquerader ever since the days of Jupiter.

COACHMAN. Aye, aye;—I guessed there was a lady in the case: but pray, why does your master pass only for *Ensign?* Now if he had shammed *General,* indeed——

FAG. Ah! Thomas, there lies the mystery o' the matter. Hark'ee, Thomas, my master is in love with a lady of a very singular taste: a lady who likes him better as a *half-pay Ensign* than if she knew he was son and heir to Sir Anthony Absolute, a baronet of three thousand a year!

COACHMAN. That is an odd taste indeed!—but has she got the stuff, Mr. Fag? is she rich, hey?

FAG. Rich!—why, I believe she owns half the stocks—Z——ds! Thomas, she could pay the national debt as easily as I could my washerwoman! She has a lapdog that eats out of gold—she feeds her parrot with small pearls—and all her thread-papers are made of bank-notes!

COACHMAN. Bravo!—Faith!—Odd! I warrant she has a set of thousands at least. But does she draw kindly with the Captain?

FAG. As fond as pigeons.

COACHMAN. May one hear her name?

FAG. Miss Lydia Languish. But there is an old tough aunt in the way; though, by the bye, she has never seen my master, for he got acquainted with Miss while on a visit in Gloucestershire.

COACHMAN. Well—I wish they were once harnessed together in matrimony.——But pray, Mr. Fag, what kind of a place is this Bath? I ha' heard a deal of it—here's a mort o' merry-making, hey?

With this preparation, the affair of Ensign Beverley and Lydia Languish is in train: the inciting force, love; the complication, a tough old aunt and a hasty father named Absolute.

The *inciting force* is the first part of the exposition which is dynamic—that is, which contains a challenge, threat, or danger to the condition of the protagonist as first glimpsed. The characteristic most inciting forces have in common is that they confront the main character or protagonist with a situation he will not accept without resistance. The threat may be from an enemy or rival, from the protagonist's past, from another aspect of the protagonist's nature, from any source that arouses his will. A purposive course to defeat the threat is chosen by the protagonist. Recognizing from the preliminary situation what the inciting force is, and having seen the protagonist choose means to contest it, the reader is in a position to follow the rising action. Against Creon's edict forbidding burial for her brother is set Antigone's "I, then, will go to heap the earth above the brother whom I love." Against Othello's "True, I have married her" is set Iago's "I hate the Moor." Against Romeo's

> Is she a Capulet?
> O dear account! My Life is my foe's debt.

is set Tybalt's

> I will withdraw; but this intrusion shall
> Now seeming sweet convert to bitter gall.

The ensuing course of the action may surprise, shock or baffle the first expectation, but it will not depart from the exposition base in a way unintelligible under the conditions offered.

2. Complication, Climax, and Denouement

The *rising action*, sometimes called the *complication* because it "ties the preliminary situation into a knot," consists of the actions taken by the protagonist and by the forces against him. The rising action usually consists of incidents in pairs, a move and a countermove, the countermove producing the next move. Or each action is a consequence of the antecedent action and becomes in turn an antecedent for another consequence. The diversity of the forces that can be made to operate in a dramatic conflict, and of the dramatic effects that arise from the kind and order of the incidents, is so great that no rule can be offered except that the sequence should rise in intensity and finally resolve itself within the potential of the situation and characters. Any last-minute intervention of an unestablished force in order to extricate the protagonist from the consequences of the preceding action will mar both the probability and necessity of the action and break the spell of the dramatic present. Such interventions most often occur in comedy and melodrama: last-minute pardons from the king, unexpected inheritances from unmentioned grandmothers, deathbed confessions from unsuspected guilty parties. They are called *deus ex machina* after the old custom of lowering a god upon the stage to settle human affairs.

The *climax*, or *turning point*, is the event that determines how the conflict will end, favorably or unfavorably for the protagonist. The *denouement* or *catastrophe* presents the outcome, disposes of subplots, and gives a glimpse of a new, stable situtation.

IV

Dialogue and Action

We have said above that a character in a play appears made-up for his part and at once starts talking and acting. The talking is the dialogue, the language resource of the playwright. The acting is not only the manner of delivery of the dialogue but the entire accompanying movement, gesture, pantomime, and stage business. Dialogue itself is, in a sense, a form of action, and the talking and the accompanying action are so integrated or fused that they seem one. We shall separate them for your attention, and then combine them, for to a play reader the heart of the dramatic illusion is the realization of the fusion of dialogue and action so that each character seems to be himself, operating naturally under the circumstances of the play.

Dramatic dialogue is artfully concentrated, selected, and heightened for economy and intensity. The demands upon it in a play are many and various: it must explain, anticipate, and with the help of action execute the play story, but its existence, even with the support of dramatic conventions, depends upon its seeming to be the natural speech of particular characters. Speech is pervasively characteristic—voice, enunciation, pronunciation, accent, dialect, speech rate, vocabulary range, the fund of image-bearing knowledge revealed—all these and more attributes of speech daily tell us things about everyone we listen to.

Coming to us from a made-up character accompanied by his actions, speech is both characteristic and characterizing. In older plays the dialogue is still characteristic and characterizing, therefore natural for the time, and it conditions and directs the imagination, even by its period quality, within the circumstances of the play story. Speech is such a strong individualizing attribute that contrasts amounting to antitheses between protagonist and antagonist are often audibly reinforced by language. Richard II and Bolingbroke are men of the same class and time, as are Brutus and Marc Antony, but they are at opposite poles in speech as well as in principles.

Dialogue is supported constantly by its physical accompaniment, action, by movement, and in the total scene, by the settings or scenery. Characters in a play are seldom stationary for long—an unfolding play on a stage is a carefully patterned continuity of movement. Scenes expand and contract with the addition and subtraction of characters; groups form and dissolve; attention shifts from side to side or from upstage to downstage. Characters welcome callers, speed parting guests, answer telephones, pass teacups, lose tempers, draw swords, swing fists, talking all the while. Stage business, as it is called, is an active accompaniment of and supplement to the dialogue. It may set out the speeches or overwhelm them in calculated violence and confusion, but a careful fusing of action and dialogue is the joint preoccupation of playwright, director, and actor. Reading an acting version of a play will supply reminders of the perpetual necessity of leading from one speech to the next by patterned movement, gesture, exits, and entrances to support the dialogue.

An excerpt from Sheridan's *The Rivals* and a selection from the first act of *The Second Mrs. Tanqueray* will supply some simple illustrations of the efforts of the dramatist to fuse natural and characterizing dialogue with action in dramatic situations.

In the selection from *The Rivals*, Lucy and Julia, who

have been exchanging confidences about their lovers, are surprised by the unexpected arrival of Sir Anthony Absolute and Mrs. Malaprop, the chief obstacles to the pursuit of their inclinations.

(*Enter* LUCY *in a hurry.*)

LUCY. O Ma'am, here is Sir Anthony Absolute just come home with your aunt.

LYDIA. They'll not come here—Lucy, do you watch.

(*Exit* LUCY.)

JULIA. Yet I must go. Sir Anthony does not know I am here, and if we meet, he'll detain me, to show me the town. I'll take another opportunity of paying my respects to Mrs. Malaprop, when she shall treat me, as long as she chooses, with her select words so ingeniously *misapplied*, without being *mispronounced*.

(*Re-enter* LUCY.)

LUCY. O lud! Ma'am, they are both coming upstairs.

LYDIA. Well, I'll not detain you, coz. Adieu, my dear Julia. I'm sure you are in haste to send to Faulkland. There—through my room you'll find another staircase.

JULIA. Adieu.—(*Embrace.*) (*Exit* JULIA.)

LYDIA. Here, my dear Lucy, hide these books. Quick, quick! Fling *Peregrine Pickle* under the toilet—throw *Roderick Random* into the closet—put *The Innocent Adultery* into *The Whole Duty of Man*—thrust *Lord Aimworth* under the sofa—cram *Ovid* behind the bolster—there—put *The Man of Feeling* into your pocket—so, so—now lay *Mrs. Chapone* in sight, and leave *Fordyce's Sermons* open on the table.

LUCY. Oh burn it, Ma'am! the hair-dresser has torn away as far as *Proper Pride*.

LYDIA. Never mind—open at *Sobriety*.—Fling me *Lord Chesterfield's Letters*—Now for 'em.

(*Enter* MRS. MALAPROP, *and* SIR ANTHONY ABSOLUTE.)

MRS. MALAPROP. There, Sir Anthony, there sits the deliberate simpleton who wants to disgrace her family, and lavish herself on a fellow not worth a shilling!

LYDIA. Madam, I thought you once— —

MRS. MALAPROP. You thought, Miss! I don't know any business you have to think at all. Thought does not become a young woman. But the point we would request of you is, that you will promise to forget this fellow—to illiterate him, I say, quite from your memory.

LYDIA. Ah! Madam! our memories are independent of our wills. It is not so easy to forget.

MRS. MALAPROP. But I say it is, Miss; there is nothing on earth so easy as to *forget*, if a person chooses to set about it. I'm sure I have as much forgot your poor dear uncle as if he had never existed—and I thought it my duty so to do; and let me tell you, Lydia, these violent memories don't become a young woman.

SIR ANTHONY. Why sure she won't pretend to remember what she's ordered not!—aye, this comes of her reading!

LYDIA. What crime, Madam, have I committed to be treated thus?

MRS. MALAPROP. Now don't attempt to extirpate yourself from the matter; you know I have proof controvertible of it. But tell me, will you promise to do as you're bid? Will you take a husband of your friend's choosing?

LYDIA. Madam, I must tell you plainly, that had I no preference for anyone else, the choice you have made would be my aversion.

MRS. MALAPROP. What business have you, Miss, with *preference* and *aversion*? They don't become a young woman; and you ought to know, that as both always wear off, 'tis safest in matrimony to begin with a little *aversion*. I am sure I hated your poor dear uncle before marriage as if he'd been a blackamoor —and yet, Miss, you are sensible what a wife I made!—and when it pleased heaven to release me from him, 'tis unknown what tears I shed! But suppose we were going to give you another choice, will you promise us to give up this Beverley?

LYDIA. Could I belie my thoughts so far as to give that promise, my actions would certainly as far belie my words.

MRS. MALAPROP. Take yourself to your room. You are fit company for nothing but your own ill-humours.

LYDIA. Willingly, Ma'am—I cannot change for the worse.

(*Exit* LYDIA.)

MRS. MALAPROP. There's a little intricate hussy for you!

SIR ANTHONY. It is not to be wondered at, Ma'am—all this is the natural consequence of teaching girls to read. Had I a thousand daughters, by heaven! I'd as soon have them taught the black art as their alphabet!

MRS. MALAPROP. Nay, nay, Sir Anthony, you are an absolute misanthropy.

SIR ANTHONY. In my way hither, Mrs. Malaprop, I observed your niece's maid coming forth from a circulating library! She had a book in each hand—they were half-bound volumes, with marble covers! From that moment I guessed how full of duty I should see her mistress!

MRS. MALAPROP. Those are vile places, indeed!

SIR ANTHONY. Madam, a circulating library in a town is as an evergreen tree of diabolical knowledge! It blossoms through the year! And depend on it, Mrs. Malaprop, that they who are so fond of handling the leaves, will long for the fruit at last.

MRS. MALAPROP. Fie, fie, Sir Anthony, you surely speak laconically!

SIR ANTHONY. Why, Mrs. Malaprop, in moderation, now, what would you have a woman know?

MRS. MALAPROP. Observe me, Sir Anthony. I would by no means wish a daughter of mine to be a progeny of learning; I don't think so much learning becomes a young woman; for instance—I would never let her meddle with Greek, or Hebrew, or Algebra, or

Simony, or Fluxions, or Paradoxes, or such inflammatory branches of learning—neither would it be necessary for her to handle any of your mathematical, astronomical, diabolical instruments;—but, Sir Anthony, I would send her, at nine years old, to a boarding-school, in order to learn a little ingenuity and artifice. Then, Sir, she should have a supercilious knowledge in accounts—and as she grew up, I would have her instructed in geometry, that she might know something of the contagious countries —but above all, Sir Anthony, she should be mistress of orthodoxy, that she might not misspell, and mispronounce words so shamefully as girls usually do; and likewise that she might reprehend the true meaning of what she is saying. This, Sir Anthony, is what I would have a woman know—and I don't think there is a superstitious article in it.

Here, in a comedy with a love-under-difficulties plot, is the first appearance of Sir Anthony Absolute and Mrs. Malaprop, who have been indirectly characterized previously, the first as "hasty in everything" and the second as "an old tough aunt in the way." Julia's remarks, as she exits, about Mrs. Malaprop's ingenious misapplication of words, are addressed in part to the audience and prepare for that singularity. Lydia's spunky resourcefulness in deceit is shown by the disposition of the books, in a violent outburst of activity—fling, throw, thrust, cram—accompanied by a list of titles that direct satirical laughter at the popular novels of the day. In one brief encounter, the three characters are sorted out as two against one, but against a clever one; a cross intrigue is hinted at; and three characterizing speech mannerisms are exhibited.

Turn now to the passage in *The Second Mrs. Tanqueray* (page 51), beginning (MORSE *enters, closing the door behind him carefully.*), and read through Paula's "What next will you think of me?"

Here the printed play is careful to include certain basic specifications of movement and action, as well as indications of the actions with which certain speeches are fused: Morse closing the door carefully and speaking hesitantly; Aubrey accepting his servant's suggestion angrily, between his teeth; Drummle prolonging his adieux by putting on a neck-handkerchief. All of this brings us closer to the sudden heightening of the situation by Paula's entrance, in superb evening dress, throwing her arms around Aubrey's neck and seating herself at the table. The animation of the scene is chiefly in the actions. The situation is forwarded by Paula's confirming what has been hinted about her, by her disregard of appearances and by her ideas—that servants are only machines, that she loves fruit when it is expensive—and by Morse's calling Aubrey's attention to his letters. The contrast between Paula's character and Aubrey's is reinforced by his "richly and tastefully decorated room" in the Albany and by their language levels.

In both of these illustrative scenes, uncomplicated and low-pitched as they are, the reader is reminded of movement, given a chance to hear dialogue as action, and invited to fill in the full scene. The constant fusing of dialogue and action in the reader's mind as he sees and hears what he reads is what "lifts" the play, endows it with movement, shapes an active imaginative equivalent, and so enriches its significance and meaning.

V

Reading the First Act

At this point we offer the first act of *The Second Mrs. Tanqueray*, 1893, by Sir Arthur Wing Pinero, an English follower of Ibsen, as an exercise in rehearsal of some of the assistance we have tried to offer the play reader thus far. We have suggested that as compared with the spectator he is at his greatest disadvantage during the first act, and especially early in the first act, when exposition is being supplied rapidly in two directions—backward to fill in the preliminary situation and forward into the rising action. We have suggested that the reader start slowly, responding to the title, date, type of play, the stage directions, and cast of characters, in order to catch up with the spectator who can see and hear. If the reader can quickly adopt the dramatically probable world so suggested, place the characters, detect the ones the play is really going to be about, and so respond to the inciting force that initiates the complication, the structural lead and the pull of the dramatic present will guide him through most plays. Our first act is not from a great play but from a good one for its time. It has a careful and clear first act, conventional but resourceful in expository methods.

from

THE SECOND MRS. TANQUERAY

Sir Arthur Wing Pinero
1855–1934

CHARACTERS

AUBREY TANQUERAY.	CAPTAIN HUGH ARDALE.
PAULA.	GORDON JAYNE, M.D.
ELLEAN.	FRANK MISQUITH, Q.C., M.P.
CAYLEY DRUMMLE.	SIR GEORGE ORREYED, BART.
MRS. CORTELYON.	LADY ORREYED.

MORSE.

TIME: *The present day* [1893].

SCENE: *The Scene of the First Act is laid at* MR. TANQUERAY's *rooms, No. 2x, The Albany, in the month of November; the occurrences of the succeeding Acts take place at his house, "Highercoombe," near Willowmere, Surrey, during the early part of the following year.*

ACT I

(AUBREY TANQUERAY's *chambers in The Albany—a richly and tastefully decorated room, elegantly and luxuriously furnished: on the right a large pair of doors opening into another room, on the left at the further end of the room a small door leading to a bedchamber. A circular table is laid for a dinner for four persons, which has now reached the stage of dessert and coffee. Everything in the apartment suggests wealth and refinement. The fire is burning brightly.*)

(AUBREY TANQUERAY, MISQUITH, *and* JAYNE *are seated at the dinner table.* AUBREY *is forty-two, handsome, winning in manner, his speech and bearing retaining some of the qualities of young manhood.* MISQUITH *is about forty-seven, genial and portly.* JAYNE *is a year or two* MISQUITH's

senior; soft-speaking and precise—in appearance a type
of the prosperous town physician. MORSE, AUBREY'S
servant, places a little cabinet of cigars and the spirit-
lamp on the table beside AUBREY, *and goes out.*)

MIS. Aubrey, it is a pleasant yet dreadful fact to con-
template, but it's nearly fifteen years since I first
dined with you. You lodged in Piccadilly in those
days, over a hat-shop. Jayne, I met you at that dinner,
and Cayley Drummle.

JAYNE. Yes, yes. What a pity it is that Cayley isn't here
to-night.

AUB. Confound the old gossip! His empty chair has
been staring us in the face all through dinner. I
ought to have told Morse to take it away.

MIS. Odd, his sending no excuse.

AUB. I'll walk round to his lodgings later on and ask
after him.

MIS. I'll go with you.

JAYNE. So will I.

AUB. (*opening the cigar-cabinet.*) Doctor, it's useless to
tempt you, I know. Frank—(MISQUITH *and* AUBREY
smoke). I particularly wished Cayley Drummle to
be one of us to-night. You two fellows and Cayley
are my closest, my best friends—

MIS. My dear Aubrey!

JAYNE. I rejoice to hear you say so.

AUB. And I wanted to see the three of you round this
table. You can't guess the reason.

MIS. You desired to give us a most excellent dinner.

JAYNE. Obviously.

AUB. (*hesitatingly*). Well—I—(*glancing at the clock*).—
Cayley won't turn up now.

JAYNE. H'm, hardly.

AUB. Then you two shall hear it. Doctor, Frank, this is
the last time we are to meet in these rooms.

JAYNE. The last time?

MIS. You're going to leave the Albany?

AUB. Yes. You've heard me speak of a house I built in the
country years ago, haven't you?

Mis. In Surrey.

Aub. Well, when my wife died I cleared out of that house and let it. I think of trying the place again.

Mis. But you'll go raving mad if ever you find yourself down there alone.

Aub. Ah, but I shan't be alone, and that's what I wanted tell you. I'm going to be married.

Jayne. Going to be married?

Mis. Married?

Aub. Yes—to-morrow.

Jayne. To-morrow?

Mis. You take my breath away! My dear fellow, I—I— of course, I congratulate you.

Jayne. And—and—so do I—heartily.

Aub. Thanks—thanks.

(*There is a moment or two of embarrassment.*)

Mis. Er—ah—this is an excellent cigar.

Jayne. Ah—um—your coffee is remarkable.

Aub. Look here; I dare say you two old friends think this treatment very strange, very unkind. So I want you to understand me. You know a marriage often cools friendships. What's the usual course of things? A man's engagement is given out, he is congratulated, complimented upon his choice; the church is filled with troops of friends, and he goes away happily to a chorus of good wishes. He comes back, sets up house in town or country, and thinks to resume the old associations, the old companionships. My dear Frank, my dear good doctor, it's very seldom that it can be done. Generally, a worm has begun to eat its way into those hearty, unreserved, prenuptial friend- ships; a damnable constraint sets in and acts like a wasting disease; and so, believe me, in nine cases out of ten a man's marriage severs for him more close ties than it forms.

Mis. Well, my dear Aubrey, I earnestly hope—

Aub. I know what you're going to say, Frank. I hope so, too. In the meantime let's face dangers. I've reminded you of the *usual* course of things, but my marriage isn't even the conventional sort of marriage likely to satisfy society. Now, Cayley's a bachelor, but you two men have wives. By the bye, my love to Mrs. Misquith and to Mrs. Jayne when you get home—don't forget that. Well, your wives may not—like—the lady I'm going to marry.

JAYNE. Aubrey, forgive me for suggesting that the lady you are going to marry may not like our wives— mine at least; I beg your pardon, Frank.

AUB. Quite so; then I must go the way my wife goes.

MIS. Come, come, pray don't let us anticipate that either side will be called upon to make such a sacrifice.

AUB. Yes, yes, let us anticipate it. And let us make up our minds to have no slow bleeding to death of our friendship. We'll end a pleasant chapter here to-night, and after to-night start afresh. When my wife and I settle down at Willowmere it's possible that we shall all come together. But if this isn't to be, for Heaven's sake let us recognize that it is simply because it *can't* be, and not wear hypocritical faces and suffer and be wretched. Doctor, Frank—(*holding out his hands, one to* MISQUITH, *the other to* JAYNE)—good luck to all of us!

MIS. But—but—do I understand we are to ask nothing? Not even the lady's name, Aubrey?

AUB. The lady, my dear Frank, belongs to the next chapter, and in that her name is Mrs. Aubrey Tanqueray.

JAYNE. (*raising his coffee-cup*). Then, in an old-fashioned way, I propose a toast. Aubrey, Frank, I give you "'The Next Chapter!"

(*They drink the toast, saying, "The Next Chapter!"*)

AUB. Doctor, find a comfortable chair; Frank, you too. As we're going to turn out by and by, let me scribble a couple of notes now while I think of them.

MIS. *and* JAYNE. Certainly—yes, yes.

AUB. It might slip my memory when I get back.

(AUBREY *sits at a writing-table at the other end of the room, and writes.*)

JAYNE (*to* MISQUITH *in a whisper*). Frank—(MISQUITH *quietly leaves his chair, and sits nearer to* JAYNE.) What is all this? Simply a morbid crank of Aubrey's with regard to ante-nuptial acquaintances?

MIS. H'm! Did you notice *one* expression he used?

JAYNE. Let me think—

MIS. "My marriage is not even the conventional sort of marriage likely to satisfy society."

JAYNE. Bless me, yes! What does that suggest?

MIS. That he has a particular rather than a general reason for anticipating estrangement from his friends, I'm afraid.

JAYNE. A horrible *mésalliance!* A dairy-maid who has given him a glass of milk during a day's hunting, or a little anaemic shopgirl! Frank, I'm utterly wretched!

MIS. My dear Jayne, speaking in absolute confidence, I have never been more profoundly depressed in my life.

(MORSE *enters.*)

MORSE (*announcing*). Mr. Drummle.

(CAYLEY DRUMMLE *enters briskly. He is a neat little man of about five-and-forty, in manner bright, airy, debonair, but with an undercurrent of seriousness.* MORSE *retires.*)

DRUM. I'm in disgrace; nobody realizes that more thoroughly than I do. Where's my host?

AUB. (*who has risen*). Cayley.

DRUM. (*shaking hands with him*). Don't speak to me till I have tendered my explanation. A harsh word from anybody would unman me.

(MISQUITH *and* JAYNE *shake hands with* DRUMMLE.)

Aub. Have you dined?

Drum. No—unless you call a bit of fish, a cutlet, and a pancake dining.

Aub. Cayley, this is disgraceful.

Jayne. Fish, a cutlet, and a pancake will require a great deal of explanation.

Mis. Especially the pancake. My dear friend, your case looks miserably weak.

Drum. Hear me! hear me!

Jayne. Now then!

Mis. Come!

Aub. Well!

Drum. It so happens that to-night I was exceptionally early in dressing for dinner.

Mis. For which dinner—the fish and cutlet?

Drum. For *this* dinner, of course—really, Frank! At a quarter to eight, in fact, I found myself trimming my nails, with ten minutes to spare. Just then enter my man with a note—would I hasten, as fast as cab could carry me, to old Lady Orreyed in Bruton Street?—"sad trouble." Now, recollect, please, I had ten minutes on my hands, old Lady Orreyed was a very dear friend of my mother's, and was in some distress.

Aub. Cayley, come to the fish and cutlet!

Mis. and Jayne. Yes, yes, and the pancake.

Drum. Upon my word! Well, the scene in Bruton Street beggars description; the women servants looked scared, the men drunk; and there was poor old Lady Orreyed on the floor of her boudoir like Queen Bess among her pillows.

Aub. What's the matter?

Drum. (*to everybody*). You know George Orreyed?

Mis. Yes.

Jayne. I've met him.

Drum. Well, he's a thing of the past.

Aub. Not dead!

Drum. Certainly, in the worst sense. He's married Mable Hervey.

Mis. What?

DRUM. It's true—this morning. The poor mother shows me his letter—a dozen curt words, and some of those ill-spelt.

MIS. (*walking up to the fireplace*). I'm very sorry.

JAYNE. Pardon my ignorance—who *was* Mable Hervey?

DRUM. You don't—? Oh, of course not. Miss Hervey—Lady Orreyed, as she now is—was a lady who would have been, perhaps has been, described in the reports of the Police or the Divorce Court as an actress. Had she belonged to a lower stratum of our advanced civilization she would, in the event of judicial inquiry, have defined her calling with equal justification as that of a dress-maker. To do her justice, she is a type of a class which is immortal. Physically, by the strange caprice of creation, curiously beautiful; mentally, she lacks even the strength of deliberate viciousness. Paint her portrait, it would symbolize a creature perfectly patrician; lance a vein of her superbly-modelled arm, you would get the poorest *vin ordinaire!* Her affections, emotions, impulses, her very existence—a burlesque! Flaxen, five-and-twenty, and feebly frolicsome; anybody's, in less gentle society I should say everybody's, property! That, doctor, was Miss Hervey who is the new Lady Orreyed. Dost thou like the picture?

MIS. Very good, Cayley! Bravo!

AUB. (*laying his hand on* DRUMMLE'S *shoulder*). You'd scarcely believe it, Jayne, but none of us really know anything about this lady, our gay young friend here, I suspect, least of all.

DRUM. Aubrey, I applaud your chivalry.

AUB. And perhaps you'll let me finish a couple of letters which Frank and Jayne have given me leave to write. (*Returning to the writing-table.*) Ring for what you want, like a good fellow!

(AUBREY *resumes his writing.*)

MIS. (*to* DRUMMLE). Still, the fish and the cutlet remain unexplained.

DRUM. Oh, the poor old woman was so weak that I insisted upon her taking some food, and felt there was
nothing for it but to sit down opposite her. The
fool! the blackguard!

MIS. Poor Orreyed! Well, he's gone under for a time.

DRUM. For a time! My dear Frank, I tell you he has
absolutely ceased to be.

(AUBREY, *who has been writing busily, turns his head
towards the speakers and listens. His lips are set, and
there is a frown upon his face.*)

For all practical purposes you may regard him as the
late George Orreyed. To-morrow the very charac-
teristics of his speech, as we remember them, will
have become obsolete.

JAYNE. But surely, in the course of years, he and his wife
will outlive—

DRUM. No, no, doctor, don't try to upset one of my
settled beliefs. You may dive into many waters, but
there is *one* social Dead Sea—!

JAYNE. Perhaps you're right.

DRUM. Right! Good God! I wish you could prove me
otherwise! Why, for years I've been sitting, and
watching and waiting.

MIS. You're in form to-night, Cayley. May we ask where
you've been in the habit of squandering your useful
leisure?

DRUM. Where? On the shore of that same sea.

MIS. And, pray, what have you been waiting for?

DRUM. For some of my best friends to come up.
(AUBREY *utters a half-stifled exclamation of im-
patience; then he hurriedly gathers up his papers
from the writing-table The three men turn to him.*)
Eh?

AUB. Oh, I—I'll finish my letters in the other room if
you'll excuse me for five minutes. Tell Cayley the
news.

(*He goes out.*)

DRUM. (*hurrying to the door*). My dear fellow, my jabbering has disturbed you! I'll never talk again as long as I live!

MIS. Close the door, Cayley.

(DRUMMLE *shuts the door.*)

JAYNE. Cayley—

DRUM. (*advancing to the dinner table*). A smoke, a smoke, or I perish! (*Selects a cigar from the little cabinet.*)

JAYNE. Cayley, marriages are in the air.

DRUM. Are they? Discover the bacillus, doctor, and destroy it.

JAYNE. I mean, among our friends.

DRUM. Oh, Nugent Warrinder's engagement to Lady Alice Tring. I've heard of that. They're not to be married till the spring.

JAYNE. Another marriage that concerns us a little takes place to-morrow.

DRUM. Whose marriage?

JAYNE. Aubrey's.

DRUM. Aub—! (*Looking towards* MISQUITH.) Is it a joke?

MIS. No.

DRUM. (*looking from* MISQUITH *to* JAYNE. To whom?

MIS. He doesn't tell us.

JAYNE. We three were asked here to-night to receive the announcement. Aubrey has some theory that marriage is likely to alienate a man from his friends, and it seems to me he has taken the precaution to wish us good-bye.

MIS. No, no.

JAYNE. Practically, surely.

DRUM. (*thoughtfully*). Marriage in general, does he mean, or *this* marriage?

JAYNE. That's the point. Frank says—

MIS. No, no, no; I feared it suggested—

JAYNE. Well, well. (*To* DRUMMLE.) What do you think of it?

DRUM. *(after a slight pause)*. Is there a light there? *(Lighting his cigar.)* He—wraps the lady—in mystery—you say?

MIS. Most modestly.

DRUM. Aubrey's—not—a very—young man.

JAYNE. Forty-three.

DRUM. Ah! *L'age critique!*

MIS. A dangerous age—yes, yes.

DRUM. When you two fellows go home, do you mind leaving me behind here?

MIS. Not at all.

JAYNE. By all means.

DRUM. All right. *(Anxiously.)* Deuce take it, the man's second marriage mustn't be another mistake! *(With his head bent he walks up to the fireplace.)*

JAYNE. You knew him in his short married life, Cayley. Terribly unsatisfactory, wasn't it?

DRUM. Well—*(looking at the door)*. I quite closed that door?

MIS. Yes. *(Settles himself on the sofa; JAYNE is seated in an arm-chair.)*

DRUM. *(smoking with his back to the fire)*. He married a Miss Herriott; that was in the year eighteen—confound dates—twenty years ago. She was a lovely creature—by Jove, she was; by religion a Roman Catholic. She was one of your cold sort, you know —all marble arms and black velvet. I remember her with painful distinctness as the only woman who ever made me nervous.

MIS. Ha, ha!

DRUM. He loved her—to distraction, as they say. Jupiter, how fervently that poor devil courted her! But I don't believe she allowed him even to squeeze her fingers. She *was* an iceberg! As for kissing, the mere contact would have given him chapped lips. However, he married her and took her away, the latter greatly to my relief.

JAYNE. Abroad, you mean?

DRUM. Eh? Yes. I imagine he gratified her by renting a villa in Lapland, but I don't know. After a while they returned, and then I saw how woefully Aubrey had miscalculated results.

JAYNE. Miscalculated—?

DRUM. He had reckoned, poor wretch, that in the early days of marriage she would thaw. But she didn't. I used to picture him closing his doors and making up the fire in the hope of seeing her features relax. Bless her, the thaw never set in! I believe she kept a thermometer in her stays and always registered ten degrees below zero. However, in time a child came— a daughter.

JAYNE. Didn't that—?

DRUM. Not a bit of it; it made matters worse. Frightened at her failure to stir up in him some sympathetic religious belief, she determined upon strong measures with regard to the child. He opposed her for a miserable year or so, but she wore him down, and the insensible little brat was placed in a convent, first in France, then in Ireland. Not long afterwards the mother died, strangely enough, of fever, the only warmth, I believe, that ever came to that woman's body.

MIS. Don't, Cayley!

JAYNE. The child is living, we know.

DRUM. Yes, if you choose to call it living. Miss Tanqueray—a young woman of nineteen now—is in the Loretto convent at Armagh. She professes to have found her true vocation in a religious life, and within a month or two will take final vows.

MIS. He ought to have removed his daughter from the convent when the mother died.

DRUM. Yes, yes, but absolutely at the end there was reconciliation between husband and wife, and she won his promise that the child should complete her conventual education. He reaped his reward. When he attempted to gain his girl's confidence and affection he was too late; he found he was dealing with the spirit of the mother. You remember his visit to Ireland last month?

JAYNE. Yes.

Drum. That was to wish his girl good-bye.

Mis. Poor fellow!

Drum. He sent for me when he came back. I think he must have had a lingering hope that the girl would relent—would come to life, as it were—at the last moment, for, for an hour or so, in this room, he was terribly shaken. I'm sure he'd clung to that hope from the persistent way in which he kept breaking off in his talk to repeat one dismal word, as if he couldn't realize his position without dinning this damned word into his head.

Jayne. What word was that?

Drum. Alone—alone.

(Aubrey *enters*.)

Aub. A thousand apologies!

Drum. (*gayly*). We are talking about you, my dear Aubrey.

(*During the telling of the story,* Misquith *has risen and gone to the fire, and* Drummle *has thrown himself full-length on the sofa.* Aubrey *now joins* Misquith *and* Jayne.)

Aub. Well, Cayley, are you surprised?

Drum. Surp—! I haven't been surprised for twenty years.

Aub. And you're not angry with me?

Drum. Angry! (*Rising.*) Because you considerately with-hold the name of a lady with whom it is now the object of my life to become acquainted? My dear fellow, you pique my curiosity, you give zest to my existence! And as for a wedding, who on earth wants to attend that familiar and probably draughty function? Ugh! My cigar's out.

Aub. Let's talk about something else.

Mis. (*looking at his watch*). Not to-night, Aubrey.

Aub. My dear Frank!

Mis. I go up to Scotland to-morrow, and there are some little matters—

JAYNE. I am off too.

AUB. No, no.

JAYNE. I must: I have to give a look to a case in Clifford Street on my way home.

AUB. (*going to the door*). Well! (MISQUITH *and* JAYNE *exchange looks with* DRUMMLE; AUBREY *opens the door and calls.*) Morse, hats and coats! I shall write to you all next week from Genoa or Florence. Now, doctor, Frank, remember, my love to Mrs. Misquith and to Mrs. Jayne!

(MORSE *enters with hats and coats.*)

MIS. *and* JAYNE. Yes, yes—yes, yes.

AUB. And your young people!

(*As* MISQUITH *and* JAYNE *put on their coats there is the clatter of careless talk.*)

JAYNE. Cayley, I meet you at dinner on Sunday.

DRUM. At the Stratfield's. That's very pleasant.

MIS. (*putting on his coat with* AUBREY's *aid*). Ah-h!

AUB. What's wrong?

MIS. A twinge. Why didn't I go to Aix in August?

JAYNE. (*shaking hands with* DRUMMLE). Good-night, Cayley.

DRUM. Good-night, my dear doctor!

MIS. (*shaking hands with* DRUMMLE). Cayley, are you in town for long?

DRUM. Dear friend, I'm nowhere for long. Good-night.

MIS. Good-night.

(AUBREY, JAYNE, *and* MISQUITH *go out, followed by* MORSE; *the hum of talk is continued outside.*)

AUB. A cigar, Frank?

MIS. No, thank you.

AUB. Going to walk, doctor?

JAYNE. If Frank will.

Mis. By all means.
Aub. It's a cold night.

(*The door is closed.* Drummle *remains standing with his coat on his arm and his hat in his hands.*)

Drum. (*to himself, thoughtfully*). Now then! What the devil!—

(Aubrey *returns.*)

Aub. (*eyeing* Drummle *a little awkwardly*). Well, Cayley?
Drum. Well, Aubrey?

(Aubrey *walks up to the fire and stands looking into it*).

Aub. You're not going, old chap?
Drum. (*sitting*). No.
Aub. (*after a slight pause, with a forced laugh*). Hah, Cayley, I never thought I should feel—shy—with you.
Drum. Why do you?
Aub. Never mind.
Drum. Now, I can quite understand a man wishing to be married in the dark, as it were.
Aub. You can?
Drum. In your place I should very likely adopt the same course.
Aub. You think so?
Drum. And if I intended marrying a lady not prominently in society, as I presume you do—as I presume you do—
Aub. Well?
Drum. As I presume you do, I'm not sure that I should tender her for preliminary dissection at afternoon tea-tables.
Aub. No?

DRUM. In fact, there is probably only one person—were
    I in your position to-night—with whom I should
    care to chat the matter over.

AUB. Who's that?

DRUM. Yourself, of course. (*Going to* AUBREY *and
    standing beside him.*) Of course, yourself, old friend.

AUB. (*after a pause*). I must seem a brute to you,
    Cayley. But there are some acts which are hard to
    explain, hard to defend—

DRUM. To defend—

AUB. Some acts which one must trust to time to put
    right.

(DRUMMLE *watches him for a moment, then takes up
his hat and coat.*)

DRUM. Well, I'll be moving.

AUB. Cayley! Confound you and your old friendship!
    Do you think I forget it? Put your coat down!
    Why did you stay behind here? Cayley, the lady I
    am going to marry is the lady—who is known as—
    Mrs. Jarman.

(*There is a pause.*)

DRUM. (*in a low voice*). Mrs. Jarman! are you serious?

(*He walks up to the fireplace, where he leans upon the
mantelpiece uttering something like a groan.*)

AUB. As you've got this out of me I give you leave to
    say all you care to say. Come, we'll be plain with
    each other. You know Mrs. Jarman?

DRUM. I first met her at—what does it matter?

AUB. Yes, yes, everything! Come!

DRUM. I met her at Homburg, two—three seasons ago.

AUB. Not as Mrs. Jarman?

DRUM. No.

AUB. She was then—?

DRUM. Mrs. Dartry.

Aub. Yes. She has also seen you in London, she says.

Drum. Certainly.

Aub. In Alford Street. Go on.

Drum. Please!

Aub. I insist.

Drum. (*with a slight shrug of the shoulders*). Some time last year I was asked by a man to sup at his house, one night after the theater.

Aub. Mr. Selwyn Ethurst—a bachelor.

Drum. Yes.

Aub. You were surprised therefore to find Mr. Ethurst aided in his cursed hospitality by a lady.

Drum. I was unprepared.

Aub. The lady you had known as Mrs. Dartry? (Drummle *inclines his head silently.*) There is something of a yachting cruise in the Mediterranean, too, is there not?

Drum. I joined Peter Jarman's yacht at Marseilles, in the Spring, a month before he died.

Aub. Mrs. Jarman was on board?

Drum. She was a kind hostess.

Aub. And an old acquaintance?

Drum. Yes.

Aub. You have told your story.

Drum. With your assistance.

Aub. I have put you to the pain of telling it to show you that this is not the case of a blind man entrapped by an artful woman. Let me add that Mrs. Jarman has no legal right to that name; that she is simply Miss Ray—Miss Paula Ray.

Drum. (*after a pause*). I should like to express my regret, Aubrey, for the way in which I spoke of George Orreyed's marriage.

Aub. You mean you compare Lady Orreyed with Miss Ray? (Drummle *is silent.*) Oh, of course! To you, Cayley, all women who have been roughly treated, and who dare to survive by borrowing a little of our philosophy, are alike. You see in the crowd of the ill-used only one pattern; you can't detect the shades of goodness, intelligence, even nobility there. Well, how should you? The crowd is dimly lighted! And, besides, yours is the way of the world.

DRUM. My dear Aubrey, I *live* in the world.

AUB. The name we give our little parish of St. James's.

DRUM. (*laying a hand on* AUBREY'S *shoulder*). And you are quite prepared, my friend, to forfeit the esteem of your little parish?

AUB. I avoid mortification by shifting from one parish to another. I give up Pall Mall for the Surrey hills; leave off varnishing my boots, and double the thickness of the soles.

DRUM. And your skin—do you double the thickness of that also?

AUB. I know you think me a fool, Cayley—you needn't infer that I'm a coward into the bargan. No! I know what I'm doing, and I do it deliberately, defiantly. I'm alone: I injure no living soul by the step I'm going to take, and so you can't urge the one argument which might restrain me. Of course, I don't expect you to think compassionately, fairly even, of the woman whom I—whom I am drawn to—

DRUM. My dear Aubrey, I assure you I consider Mrs.— Miss Jarman—Mrs. Ray—Miss Ray—delightful. But I confess there is a form of chivalry which I gravely distrust, especially in a man of—our age.

AUB. Thanks. I've heard you say that from forty till fifty a man is at heart either a stoic or a satyr.

DRUM. (*protestingly*). Ah! now—

AUB. I am neither. I have a temperate, honorable affection for Mrs. Jarman. She has never met a man who has treated her well—I intend to treat her well. That's all. And in a few years, Cayley, if you've not quite forsaken me, I'll prove to you that it's possible to rear a life of happiness, of good repute, on a—miserable foundation.

DRUM. (*offering his hand*). Do prove it!

AUB. (*taking his hand*). We have spoken too freely of —of Mrs. Jarman. I was excited—angry. Please forget it!

DRUM. My dear Aubrey, when we next meet I shall remember nothing but my respect for the lady who bears your name.

(MORSE *enters, closing the door behind him carefully.*)

AUB. What is it?

MORSE (*hesitatingly*). May I speak to you, sir? (*In an undertone.*) Mrs. Jarman, sir.

AUB. (*softly to* MORSE). Mrs. Jarman! Do you mean she is at the lodge in her carriage?

MORSE. No, sir—here. (AUBREY *looks towards* DRUM-MLE, *perplexed.*) There's a nice fire in your—in that room, sir. (*Glancing in the direction of the door leading to the bedroom.*)

AUB. (*between his teeth, angrily*). Very well.

(MORSE *retires.*)

DRUM. (*looking at his watch*). A quarter to eleven—horrible! (*Taking up his hat and coat.*) Must get to bed—up late every night this week. (AUBREY *assists* DRUMMLE *with his coat.*) Thank you. Well, good-night, Aubrey. I feel I've been dooced serious, quite out of keeping with myself; pray overlook it.

AUB. (*kindly*). Ah, Cayley!

DRUM. (*putting on a neck-handerchief*). And remember that, after all, I'm merely a spectator in life; nothing more than a man at a play, in fact; only, like the old-fashioned playgoer, I love to see certain characters happy and comfortable at the finish. You understand?

AUB. I think I do.

DRUM. Then, for as long as you can, old friend, will you —keep a stall for me?

AUB. Yes, Cayley.

DRUM. (*gayly*). Ah, ha! Good-night! (*Bustling to the door.*) Don't bother! I'll let myself out! Good-night! God bless yer!

(*He goes out;* AUBREY *follows him.* MORSE *enters by the other door, carrying some unopened letters, which*

*after a little consideration he places on the mantelpiece
against the clock.* AUBREY *returns.*)

AUB. Yes?

MORSE. You hadn't seen your letters that came by the
nine o'clock post, sir; I've put 'em where they'll
catch your eye by and by.

AUB. Thank you.

MORSE (*hesitatingly*). Gunter's cook and waiter have
gone, sir. Would you prefer me to go to bed?

AUB. (*frowning*). Certainly not.

MORSE. Very well, sir.

(*He goes out.*)

AUB. (*opening the upper door*). Paula! Paula!

(PAULA *enters and throws her arms round his neck.
She is a young woman of about twenty-seven: beautiful,
fresh, innocent-looking. She is in superb evening dress.*)

PAULA. Dearest!

AUB. Why have you come here?

PAULA. Angry?

AUB. Yes—no. But it's eleven o'clock.

PAULA (*laughing*). I know.

AUB. What on earth will Morse think?

PAULA. Do you trouble yourself about what servants
think?

AUB. Of course.

PAULA. Goose! They're only machines made to wait upon
people—and to give evidence in the Divorce Court.
(*Looking round.*) Oh, indeed! A snug little dinner!

AUB. Three men.

PAULA (*suspiciously*). Men?

AUB. Men.

PAULA (*penitently*). Ah! (*Sitting at the table.*) I'm so
hungry.

AUB. Let me get you some game pie, or some—

PAULA. No, no, hungry for this. What beautiful fruit!

I love fruit when it's expensive. (*He clears a space on the table, places a plate before her, and helps her to fruit.*) I haven't dined, Aubrey dear.

Aub. My poor girl! Why?

Paula. In the first place, I forgot to order any dinner, and my cook, who has always loathed me, thought he'd pay me out before he departed.

Aub. The beast!

Paula. That's precisely what I—

Aub. No, Paula!

Paula. What I told my maid to call him. What next will you think of me?

Aub. Forgive me. You must be starved.

Paula (*eating fruit*). I didn't care. As there was nothing to eat, I sat in my best frock, with my toes on the dining-room fender, and dreamt, oh, such a lovely dinner party.

Aub. Dear lonely little woman!

Paula. It was perfect. I saw you at the end of a very long table, opposite me, and we exchanged sly glances now and again over the flowers. We were host and hostess, Aubrey, and had been married about five years.

Aub. (*kissing her hand*). Five years.

Paula. And on each side of us was the nicest set imaginable—you know, dearest, the sort of men and women that can't be imitated.

Aub. Yes, yes. Eat some more fruit.

Paula. But I haven't told you the best part of my dream.

Aub. Tell me.

Paula. Well, although we had been married only such a few years, I seemed to know by the look on their faces that none of our guests had ever heard anything —anything—anything peculiar about the fascinating hostess.

Aub. That's just how it will be, Paula. The world moves so quickly. That's just how it will be.

Paula. (*with a little grimace*). I wonder! (*Glancing at the fire.*) Ugh! Do throw another log on.

AUB. (*mending the fire.*) There! But you mustn't be
here long.

PAULA. Hospitable wretch! I've something important to
tell you. No, stay where you are. (*Turning from
him, her face averted.*) Look here, that was my
dream, Aubrey; but the fire went out while I was
dozing, and I woke up with a regular fit of the
shivers. And the result of it all was that I ran upstairs and scribbled you a letter.

AUB. Dear baby!

PAULA. Remain where you are. (*Taking a letter from her
pocket.*) This is it. I've given you an account of
myself, furnished you with a list of my adventures
since I—you know. (*Weighing the letter in her
hand.*) I wonder if it would go for a penny. Most of
it you're acquainted with; *I've* told you a good deal,
haven't I?

AUB. Oh, Paula!

PAULA. What I haven't told you I dare say you've heard
from others. But in case they've omitted anything—
the dears—it's all here.

AUB. In Heaven's name, why must you talk like this
to-night?

PAULA. It may save discussion by and by, don't you
think? (*Holding out the letter.*) There you are.

AUB. No, dear, no.

PAULA. Take it. (*He takes the letter.*) Read it through
after I've gone, and then—read it again, and turn
the matter over in your mind finally. And if, even
at the very last moment, you feel you—oughtn't
to go to church with me, send a messenger to Pont
Street, any time before eleven to-morrow, telling me
that you're afraid, and I—I'll take the blow.

AUB. Why, what—what do you think I am?

PAULA. That's it. It's because I know you're such a dear
good fellow that I want to save you the chance of
ever feeling sorry you married me. I really love
you so much, Aubrey, that to save you that, I'd
rather you treated me as—as the others have done.

AUB. (*turning from her with a cry*). Oh!

PAULA. (*after a slight pause*). I suppose I've shocked you.
   I can't help it if I have.

(*She sits with assumed languor and indifference. He
turns to her, advances, and kneels by her.*)

AUB. My dearest, you don't understand me. I—I can't
   bear to hear you always talking about—what's done
   with. I tell you I'll never remember it; Paula, can't
   you dismiss it? Try. Darling, if we promise each
   other to forget, to forget, we're bound to be happy.
   After all, it's a mechanical matter; the moment a
   wretched thought enters your head, you quickly
   think of something bright—it depends on one's
   will. Shall I burn this, dear? (*Referring to the letter
   he holds in his hand.*) Let me, let me!
PAULA (*with a shrug of the shoulders*). I don't suppose
   there's much that's new to you in it—just as you
   like.

(*He goes to the fire, burns the letter.*)

AUB. There's an end of it. (*Returning to her.*) What's
   the matter?
PAULA (*rising coldly*). Oh, nothing! I'll go and put my
   cloak on.
AUB. (*detaining her*). What *is* the matter?
PAULA. Well, I think you might have said, "You're very
   generous, Paula," or at least, "Thank you, dear,"
   when I offered to set you free.
AUB. (*catching her in his arms*). Ah!
PAULA. Ah! ah! Ha! ha. It's all very well, but you don't
   know what it cost me to make such an offer. I do so
   want to be married.
AUB. But you never imagined—?
PAULA. Perhaps not. And yet I *did* think of what I'd do
   at the end of our acquaintance if you had preferred
   to behave like the rest. (*Taking a flower from her
   bodice.*)
AUB. Hush!

PAULA. Oh, I forgot!

AUB. What would you have done when we parted?

PAULA. Why, killed myself.

AUB. Paula, dear!

PAULA. It's true. (*Putting the flower in his buttonhole.*) Do you know, I feel certain I should make away with myself if anything serious happened to me.

AUB. Anything serious! What, has nothing ever been serious to you, Paula?

PAULA. Not lately; not since a long while ago. I made up my mind then to have done with taking things seriously. If I hadn't, I— However, we won't talk about that.

AUB. But now, now, life will be different to you, won't it—quite different? Eh, dear?

PAULA. Oh, yes, now. Only, Aubrey, mind you keep me always happy.

AUB. I will try to.

PAULA. I know I couldn't swallow a second big dose of misery. I know that if ever I felt wretched again—truly wretched—I should take a leaf out of Connie Tirlemont's book. You remember? They found her— (*With a look of horror.*)

AUB. For God's sake, don't let your thoughts run on such things!

PAULA (*laughing*). Ha, ha, how scared you look! There, think of the time! Dearest, what will my coachman say? My cloak!

(*She runs off, gayly, by the upper door.* AUBREY *looks after her for a moment, then he walks up to the fire and stands warming his feet at the bars. As he does so he raises his head and observes the letters upon the mantelpiece. He takes one down quickly.*)

AUB. Ah! Ellean! (*Opening the letter and reading.*) "My dear father—A great change has come over me. I believe my mother in Heaven has spoken to me, and counseled me to turn to you in your loneliness. At any rate, your words have reached my heart, and

I no longer feel fitted for this solemn life. I am
ready to take my place by you. Dear father, will
you receive me?—ELLEAN."

(PAULA *reënters, dressed in a handsome cloak. He
stares at her as if he hardly realized her presence.*)

PAULA. What are you staring at? Don't you admire my
cloak?

AUB. Yes.

PAULA. Couldn't you wait till I'd gone before reading
your letters?

AUB. (*putting the letter away*). I beg your pardon.

PAULA. Take me downstairs to the carriage. (*Slipping her
arm through his.*) How I tease you! To-morrow! I'm
so happy!

(*They go out.*)

Now for a backward look at a first act, and first at the
amount of fact it has implanted. A half hour ago you did
not know (shall we say) that Aubrey Tanqueray existed.
You now know that he is forty-three years old and for
sixteen years a widower following an unsatisfactory marriage. He has a daughter, Ellean, nineteen, who has
recently refused to leave the convent and join him in the
world. You know that he has led a settled life in an
apartment in which everything "suggests wealth and refinement." These are "backward-looking" matters of exposition, filling out the preliminary situation.

You also know that tomorrow he is to marry Paula Ray,
a "woman with a past"; that he is deliberately destroying
his comfortable but *alone* situation; that he hopes to rear,
with Paula, a "life of happiness, of good repute, on a
miserable foundation"; and that his friends, representing
society, anticipate his failure. You have further met Paula
Ray, unexpectedly; seen Tanqueray burn her confession of
past affairs; wondered, perhaps, if one of them might not

turn up later; seen Morse "plant" the letter in which Ellean asks to be received as his daughter—a step which more luckily timed might have assuaged his aloneness; and from the cast of characters, you have noted that Lady Orreyed is to play a future part. These are "forward looking" matters of exposition, introducing the inciting force and leading into the complication.

But the summary order, as above, is far from the linear order in which these items appeared. To make such a linear order and to note the devices used would be a good lesson in first acts. Of the devices, note that dialogue is one. Expository dialogue is difficult to make natural, because two people do not usually explain to one another what they both know. Pinero has managed this, first, by opening late in the situation on the dinner at which Tanqueray had *planned* to announce his marriage to Jayne, Misquith, and Drummle. In the absence of Drummle, he announces it to Jayne and Misquith. From "Then you two shall hear it Doctor, Frank, this is the last time we are to meet in these rooms" runs a developing line through "I'm going to be married," "My marriage isn't even the conventional sort likely to satisfy society," "Your wives may not—like—the lady I'm going to marry. The total implication is restated to Drummle, following Tanqueray's "Tell Cayley the news," but not until Drummle, in ironical ignorance, has expatiated on the George Orreyed–Mable Hervey marriage and the *one* social Dead Sea, thereby emphasizing what Tanqueray's problem will be. The withdrawal of Tanqueray to the rear of the stage to write notes while Misquith and Jayne talk over his unconventional marriage, and again while Drummle tells them of Tanqueray's first marriage, looks and is awkward, in a realistic sense, but it is carried off by Tanqueray's reactions to overhearing Drummle.

Actually, efficient exposition devices are almost conventions in the support an audience gives them. The audience *wants* to get on with it. Prologues, soliloquies, the two servants, the confidant (Drummle for Tanqueray after the departure of Jayne and Misquith), remarks overheard, letters read aloud, three friends talking about a fourth—all are acceptable *early* in a play. The amount of exposition contained in one act, here, has certainly taxed Pinero's craftsmanship, but the multiple lines of anticipation make it welcome. In addition, certain themes, or portentous phrases, such as "alone—alone," "he has absolutely ceased to be," "*one* social Dead Sea," "killed myself," get into the dialogue, and connect themselves with the developing possibilities.

You have, presumably, sized up the characters, but again, to select the details and their dramatic interrelation would be a good lesson. How are you led to recognize that Tanqueray, Paula, and Ellean are the characters this play is about? How are you led to recognize that Drummle is going to be closer to the situation than Jayne and Misquith? How are you led to a conviction that Tanqueray will not succeed in rearing a life of happiness—in other words, that the play is not to be a comedy?

VI

Meaning in Drama

The meaning, or theme, of a play—that truth about human life, nature, or experience the playwright has founded his play story upon and adhered to in selecting and rejecting the psychology, language, and actions of his characters—is sometimes stated, phrased, or explicitly dramatized in the play. The play story may literally contain, and in its representation express, all that the play means. Or the play story may be a provocative, symbolic, or allusive means of leading the audience to the perception of a universal truth beyond or above its particulars. The theme of a play is often a basic truism about human nature's knowledge of itself and of the ordering of that moral world which is possible to it. Conflicts and their resolutions as precipitated between men and women, love and hate, tradition and revolt, desire and duty, passion and law, for example, stick close to our wisdom about ourselves and our universe.

The meaning of a specific play, grounded by a playwright in the unity of its subject, is seen by him to be in the total response of the audience to the story and its agents, the characters. His plotting of the story, the dialogue, and other actions of the characters are among his means of leading the reader to the meaning. He may give a clue in the title of the play: *Everyman, Ghosts, Purgatory, The Green*

Pastures, The Sins of the Fathers, Pygmalion. Within the play, action is meaningful—gesture, facial expressions, pauses, things *not* said. Dialogue also expresses the feelings, decisions, and conclusions of the characters. Sometimes the meaning is in the interaction or conjunction of the lines, or in *how* they are spoken. Sometimes the speeches are directly thematic. In problem plays or thesis plays opposing lines of argument may be obtrusive, just as opposing sides of the conflict are, but under any dramatic tension characters speak not only as agents in an action but as human beings discovering principles and convictions as a result of that action. Here the reader is at home; he has formed his opinion of the characters; he responds to what is said in terms of who is saying it and why. He can recognize the thoughts the dramatist agrees with and those he introduces to discredit. Many good things are said in dramatic dialogue in this incidental fashion, some of them by the antagonistic characters or by characters on the wrong side of the central issue.

Perception of irony by the reader also stimulates his discovery of meaning. Whenever he feels sure that two remarks are in contrast, with the truth in neither, whenever he is ahead of a character because he knows more than the character does, he is making meaning. Dramatic, or Sophoclean, irony, in which an outcome is foreknown by the reader but not by the character, directs the reader toward the meaning of the play as a whole.

The final meaning of a play, however, is the product of its total impression. In this sense, theme is structural; it is led up to and affirmed by the interaction upon the reader of all the elements of the play. A play often "stages" its final conclusion about human life; if it does not, such a conclusion will be implicitly formulated by the reader. "What fools these mortals be" is a thematic statement by Puck. "As flies to wanton boys are we to the Gods, They kill us for their sport" is a thematic statement by Lear. The total meaning, however, is not suddenly impressed upon a play in its most conclusive speech or scene, but is the product of the emphasis, repetition, language, and structural guidance of the dramatist. That *unity* which Aristotle insisted a dramatic action should have, the unity we have stressed in the sections on the nature of drama, on plot, and on tragedy, is in part, certainly, a unity of subject. All the elements of a play contribute to making it probable that its particular meaning would emerge within the characters under the conditions offered.

VII

Traditional Types of Plays

Plays, like other works of art, nourish themselves on the subjects and forms of expression that are part of the surrounding society. Plays are distinctly contemporary upon their first appearance; sometimes they are trying to lead their society, and they collide with it; sometimes they are hand in glove with the tastes, ideas, and attitudes of their day. Greek tragedies were composed and performed for a national religious festival; mystery and morality plays were created by and for the medieval world; the Elizabethans flocked to their wooden O's to see their players show "the very age and body of the time his form and pressure."

Plays are as subject to imitation as other art forms; in any period, plays like the plays then being welcomed are likely to appear. The common features of any successful type of play get assembled into something like a formula or set of rules. It is not true, of course, that two plays of the same type, whether by the same or different dramatists, are identical. The *Oedipus the King* and *Antigone* of Sophocles are not identical, though both are classical tragedies; *The Boor* and *The Proposal* of Chekhov are not identical, though both are farces. The same type of play, with the scope it affords for unified, probable, particular examples, may satisfy both dramatist and society for long periods of time.

65

Foreknowledge of the type of play he intends to create can be both a focus for the playwright's selection and combination of dramatic elements and a restraint upon his imagination. If he destroys the delicate balance between the frame and the individual creation within it the product may be rejected—and father no imitations. Audiences have been puzzled, shocked, even infuriated by elements of novelty in plays, sometimes by the ideas, sometimes by the treatment. A battle between the defenders of the traditional, neoclassical mode and enthusiasts for a new romantic mode broke out during the performance of Victor Hugo's *Hernani* in Paris in 1830. The Abbey Theatre in Dublin had been the scene of so many riots against the religious, moral, or national implications of plays that W. B. Yeats, in trying to quiet the uproar over Sean O'Casey's *The Plough and the Stars*, told the audience, "You have once more rocked the cradle of reputation." However, dramatists are often trying not only to please their age but to teach it, lead it, or advance it. They experiment, innovate, stretch or change the prevailing mode in order to say more or to say it in a new way; originality often wins after the initial shock wears off. But when elements of novelty do appear successfully in a familiar type of play, they will be noted, imitated, and formulated into rules for the new type. So by a mingled process of imitation and innovation, of model and experiment, of convention and revolt, drama progresses, keeps contemporary, keeps up with or ahead of its age. In a close study of the development of drama each emerging type in each social period is precisely defined; the degree and kind of adaptation and innovation are noted.

The recommendation of the players given by Polonius to Hamlet

> The best actors in the world, either for tragedy, comedy, history, pastoral, pastoral-comical, historical-pastoral, tragical-historical, tragical-comical-historical-pastoral, scene individable, or poem unlimited: . . .

s often taken as Shakespeare's satirical comment on tr
overminute classification of plays, but the serious studen
of dramatic literature will need to know many of them,
Polonius or no.

We offer here a division of drama into farce, comedy,
melodrama, and tragedy, according to the response in-
ended. Although drama runs the gamut from the lightest
laughter to the proudest tears, these four responses underlie
the specific types of plays in all periods. As points of refer-
ence, they will help orient the reader in any play.

A. Farce

Farce aims at laughter, provoked by outrageous assaults
on decorum and restraint. Farce uses violent or slapstick
behavior, exaggerated pantomime, clowning, absurd situa-
ions, gags, and wisecracks, usually combined in a fast-
paced uproar of cross-purposes and misunderstandings.
Situations are nonsensical or iconoclastic in farce—identical
twins mistaken for one another, the right people in the
wrong bedrooms, the "chase," in which everybody chases
everybody else without knowing why, the beating and
berating of people under false impressions, absurd marital
misunderstandings. The whole is offered for its display of
human behavior out of control. Physical impropriety and
violence are not the only means of farcing; release of re-
trictive bonds may be plotted into quiet, underplayed
displays of hilarious escapes from the fetters of decorum.
Farce has an ancient and honorable history; it is an
artistic medium when it serves its limited, but salutary,
aims with successful means. Its "thoughtless laughter" is
one response that drama seems endlessly suited to evoke. It
s difficult to name farces without trespassing upon farce-
comedy, for involvement with the characters, or relation of
the situation to a serious view of life, moves the farce out of
orbit. However, the "fine old art of farce" may, by careful

eatment of its materials, rise far above slapstick. It is an art in itself and a contributor to high comedy. Shake speare's *The Comedy of Errors*, Oscar Wilde's *The Importance of Being Earnest*, Chekhov's *The Boor* and *The Proposal*, Anatole France's *The Man Who Married a Dumb Wife*, Molière's *Scapin*, and Feydeau's *Keep an Eye on Amélie* are a few examples of farces given immortality by skillful exploitation of the resources of the type.

B. Comedy

Comedy grows out of farce by almost imperceptible gradations. The farcical element, the resort to hamming clowning, wisecracking, or wide-open absurdity to stimulate laughter, is the spice of life to many comedies. Laughter engenders laughter; a little thoughtless laughter may engender some thoughtful laughter. Light comedy or farce comedy are serviceable terms covering a wide middle band between farce and high comedy. In general, comedy presents plot situations more probable than those of farce more serious and believable, but not threatening or fatal. The characters are not the complete stereotypes that people farces; they are socially recognizable, slightly individualized; we can laugh at or with them with some concern for their predicaments. However, they do not compel our identification with them or cause us to think of grave issues through them. The laughter of comedy may be the "warm laughter" of secure and affectionate faith in the imperfect but admirable world in which good people have passing troubles with one another, as in Shakespeare's *A Midsummer Night's Dream* or *As You Like It*, Eugene O'Neill's *Ah! Wilderness*, Lindsay and Crouse's *Life with Father*. It may be the "corrective laughter" of satire, from gentle to savage, directed at a ridiculous incongruity, abnormality, or excess of a human trait, as in Molière's

Tartuffe and Ben Jonson's *Volpone*. The laughter of comedy may be laughter at wit, the epigram, the telling exchange, the contest for cleverness between sophisticated people, as in comedy of manners. Intellectual comedy, or the comedy of ideas, uses situations and characters to produce "thoughtful laughter," not on the gravest issues of life, but on irrationalities in the society. Whether overlapping with farce or extending to a vision of humor as a socially healthful force, comedy is a dramatic effect that engenders many subtypes as societies change, for it is a distinctly social mirror. All comedy is perhaps related, as the branches of a tree are related to the trunk, by being rooted in a "comic vision," a mood in which the world seems manageable, somehow, by treating its passing difficulties with a sense of humor, with gaiety, with a protective wit aimed partly at ourselves.

C. Melodrama, Drame, and Problem Play

Melodrama used as a term for a type of play applies not only to the mystery-thriller, but to plays of strong plot situations and strong emotions, full of possible but usually averted disaster for the sympathetic characters. It enlists identification rather than detachment. It often exploits "poetic justice" and engenders pity for the protagonist and hate for the antagonist. It poses serious consequences for the protagonist, but sometimes does not pose them quite honestly. They are external and will be escaped or evaded somehow.

The honest melodrama, which offers such excitements as are made possible by a few easy assumptions about the characters and about the element of chance, luck, or coincidence in solving situations, is, of course, a perfectly legitimate dramatic type that does not need to apologize for itself. The common statement that farce is to comedy what melodrama is to tragedy sometimes implies that farce and melodrama are lower forms of artistic endeavor, and from one point of view they are, but in very few periods would the theater have survived if farce and melodrama had been subtracted from it. All ages seem to like to laugh and to escape. Since both farce and melodrama produce strong reactions by visible means, they are at home in motion pictures, and their appeal there is perennial; but they often arrive on the screen from the stage.

At the top of its possibilities, melodrama overlaps with serious drama, or *drame*, and with the problem play and approaches tragedy. The problem play, which uses melodramatic effects to protest a social evil, is a serious drama with an immediate social purpose; it uses the strong emotions of melodrama to compel action. Some problem plays outlast their immediate applicability and live on the human values the problem reveals, and thus received seem to be *drame* or tragedy. The characters, again, mark the difference.

D. Tragedy

The tragic effect is the hardest of the dramatic effects to define and the one that is subjected to the greatest defining effort. So much effort, in fact, has gone into the theory of tragedy that the reader may be diverted to theory before he has enough experience with tragedies to have a foundation in his own responses. We therefore simplify in terms of the rule rather than the exceptions, and recommend postponing the refining of tragic theory until many tragedies have been read.

Tragedy represents characters whose wills are set on courses necessary to their own moral natures and who are overpowered by the forces against them. The following paragraph from Aristotle's *Poetics* (which was translated by S. H. Butcher) states the effect to be produced as pity and fear and indicates the nature of the tragic protagonist.

> A perfect tragedy should imitate actions which excite pity and fear, this being the distinctive function of tragic imitation. It follows plainly, in the first place, that the change of fortune presented must not be the spectacle of a virtuous man brought from prosperity to adversity, for this moves neither pity nor fear; it merely shocks us. Nor, again, that of a bad man passing from adversity to prosperity, for nothing can be more alien to the spirit of Tragedy; it possesses no single tragic quality; it neither satisfies the moral sense nor calls forth pity or fear. Nor, again, should the downfall of an utter villain be exhibited. A plot of this kind would doubtless satisfy the moral sense, but it would inspire neither pity nor fear; for pity is aroused by unmerited misfortune, fear by the misfortune of a man like ourselves. Such an event, therefore, will be neither pitiful nor terrible. There remains, then, the character between these two extremes—that of a man who is not eminently good and just, yet whose misfortune is brought about not by vice or depravity, but by some error or frailty. He must be one who is highly renowned and prosperous—a personage like Oedipus, Thyestes, or other illustrious men of such families.

The tragic protagonist, by the strength of his will, the sincerity of his choice of a course of action, and the strenuousness of his efforts, compels extreme identification. We pity the impotence of the highest human powers in an imperfect individual imbued with them, and watch fearfully while forces stronger than such a protagonist overwhelm him. His destruction is inescapable, unacceptable, and should produce a painful resentment at the moral imperfection or poetic injustice in the universe.

Instead, tragedy "through pity and fear effects the proper katharsis of those emotions." Aristotle's phrase has been analyzed through the centuries; does *katharsis* mean "purgation," or does it mean "purification"; does it mean to empty the mind of the spectator of pity and fear or to raise the mind above them, replace them by exaltation, admiration, reconciliation?

The tragic protagonist contests the external and dramatically visible forces arrayed against him, but this visible and particular contest is only an outward representation of his internal conflict. He has responded to a compelling moral challenge by a decision reached alone. He often answers to his defeat with a defiant affirmation of the rightness of his choice. Under the particulars of any tragedy lies the universal principle that soul-searching catastrophes are a part of the human situation in a universe not committed to indulging the individual will. Individuals who have power to defy and rise above the catastrophic repudiation of their wills exalt mankind.

The effects of tragedy being the most profound and elevating of all dramatic effects, and the achievement of tragedy the highest reach of dramatic art, it is natural that dramatic criticism concentrates on the nature, laws, and purity of tragedy. Tragedy that passes the most exacting tests is rare. In his *The Anatomy of Drama*, Alan Reynolds Thompson finds only three eras in which great tragedies have been produced: in Athens in the fifth century B.C., in Elizabethan England, and in the Paris of Louis XIV. He then lists twenty supreme tragedies for all the centuries represented, with none after Racine, although Ibsen's *Ghosts* would be his next choice.

As noted above, the interplay between the theater and its society is very close; the possibility or impossibility of achieving supreme tragedies has therefore been used as a test for societies. Currently we are debating whether little men rather than highly renowned men are possible tragic protagonists, whether the modern world is capable of producing true tragedies, whether we have a sense of a moral order to ground them in.

However, the acute dissection of tragedy should follow

upon an acquaintance with many of them; with, say, the twenty in Professor Thompson's list. A slightly less than supreme tragedy is still a wonderfully rewarding play to read, and the "foothills of tragedy," which slope down from the lofty peaks to the plain of ordinary melodrama, are well worth exploring also.

Viewed structurally, tragedies vindicate fully the causal plot structure we have sketched, since inevitability must be demonstrated out of challenge and response to force us to accept the tragic outcome. They are unified, made probable and inevitable, by harmonizing a strong character, capable of searching and revealing emotions we can identify as universal, with a tragic world which declares through tone, spectacle, language, and action that it is antagonistic, violent, and destructive. We enter into the kind of pity and fear which will lead to purgation of those emotions through extreme identification or empathy with the protagonist. We contest his fate, and so will accept no easy means or artificial circumstances. The plot does govern a tragedy, but the illusion that we are watching people acting as they must, having their moral natures, being themselves in their circumstances, must survive our own desire to break with the illusion. The inevitability of defeat under the conditions offered, and the recognition of internal triumph in external defeat, are the two fused elements in the tragic effect.

VIII

Modern Plays

Until modern times, the playwright's efforts were governed by unifying the elements of drama to produce the effect of farce, comedy, melodrama, or tragedy in some pure or acceptably blended form. He had before him, also, a prevailing theatrical style. One theatrical style succeeded another: romantic tragedy gave way to neoclassical tragedy; neoclassical comedies gave way to realistic comedies. The whole society was permeated with the changed beliefs, tastes, and attitudes that the changing theatrical styles derived from and expressed.

The modern age, however, is not unified in acceptance of any one set of basic concepts; it has had too many shocks, too rapid an assault on the old, and too many rival claimants for the new. Roughly, the vigorous transformation of the play, the stage, and acting was directed first at greater realism, in the sense of a more exact external representation of the internal life the playwright felt his characters to have.

Naturalism is a term used for a deterministic realism, one in which the characters are the products of their environment, and the forces that play upon the characters are what the play is really about. Revelations of the conditioning of characters by heredity, economic circumstances, and the mores, codes, and loyalties of cultures, sometimes coupled with theses directed at modifying them, mark naturalistic plays. Realism in the sense of fidelity to fact or detail is a method that can be employed in plays of nondeterministic ideology.

Under the impetus toward realistic depiction of life, stage settings were made painstakingly exact replicas of the environmental envelope that had engendered the play story. The room-with-one-wall-removed concept went hand in hand with a new realistic school of ensemble acting, spreading from Konstantin Stanislavsky's directing of Chekhov's plays at the Moscow Art Theater. Ignoring the audience, each actor carried out his identity as a character, dealing with other characters in a group in a room, unaware that one wall had been removed. Dialogue and costume became realistic also.

Developments in modern drama came very rapidly once the stage set out to catch up with the previous responses of the other arts to the changed conditions in modern society. Ibsen is usually regarded as the pioneer in naturalistic treatments of middle-class lives in middle-class environments. But segments of society far below those depicted by Ibsen followed on the stage: ordinary life as lived by common people, working-class people, and down-and-out people was represented with realistic fidelity to the hovel, tenement, farmhouse, dive or water front, that was their world in such plays as Gorky's *The Lower Depths*, Rice's *Street Scene*, O'Neill's *Desire Under the Elms*, O'Casey's *Juno and the Paycock*.

Realism, whether associated with deterministic themes or not, continued as the dominant theatrical style in modern drama, but the conviction that much of the truth of life cannot be equated with its externals led to various antirealistic or presentational styles: symbolism, expressionism, theatricalism. The invisible inner life, sometimes shockingly or absurdly at variance with the objectively demonstrated product-of-forces interpretation, received dramatic expression in antirealistic ways, ways that made the invisible visible according to laws other than materialistic.

Both realism and antirealism took advantage of a series of brilliant, zealous enlargements of the possibilities of stagecraft. The stage has been made revolving, has been surrounded by spectators in arena staging, or theater in the round, has been made flexible and unlocalized. Increased command over lighting and sound has aided all the arts contributing to theater in capturing on the stage a more complete illusion of life.

Traditional drama would have been suffused with the modern cast of man, with the modern view of society, and with the effects of the new theatrical resources even if it had continued to produce farces, comedies, melodramas, and tragedies in some familiar form. But the modern playwright is himself part of the diversity and uncertainty of modern man's views of himself and his universe. He resists creating a pure or traditional effect (comedy or tragedy) and resists a single style. He blends, crosses, and combines both diverse dramatic effects and diverse theatrical styles in the same play. Perhaps the most disconcerting aspect of modern drama to audiences and readers first exposed to it was its *mixed* nature: naturalism dissolved into fantasy, every character had his own story, the brutal and the tender were juxtaposed, the most limiting realism was succeeded by symbols universalizing the implications, characters dropped from a present action into a flashback of childhood. The modern playwright, however, has not abandoned unity or harmony. By remaining free to manipulate many dramatic elements, he tries to achieve an illusion of life in a play full of its own nature, carrying its own seal of dramatic probability upon it. He is still an artificer, but one working with many more tools.

The reader encounters in antirealistic plays the same mingling of farce and pathos, of internal and external states of mind, of symbol and action, that is offered him in antirealistic fiction and poetry. The structure of conflict, however, still underlies most antirealistic plays and provides the reader with his best lead through the play. Only when language itself is subordinated or dispensed with, as in the theater of the absurd, will the reader find that the unity-of-action lead is unprofitable to follow. The various types of nonrealistic settings and the interpretative use of music and spectacle will challenge the reader's imaginative powers, but his orientation in the modern ideas and arts that underlie the new theater will be a compensating aid.

For Further Reading

A. Collections of Plays, Some with Treatments of Drama or of the Dramatists Represented

ALLISON, ALEXANDER W., ARTHUR J. CARR, and ARTHUR M. EASTMAN. *Masterpieces of the Drama.* New York: The Macmillan Company, 1957, 1966

ALTENBERND, LYNN, and LESLIE L. LEWIS (eds.). *Introduction to Literature: Plays.* New York: The Macmillan Company, 1963.

BLOCK, HASKELL M., and ROBERT G. SHEDD (eds.). *Masters of Modern Drama.* New York: Random House, 1962.

BROOKS, CLEANTH, and ROBERT B. HEILMAN. *Understanding Drama.* New York: Holt, Rinehart & Winston, 1960.

CORRIGAN, ROBERT W. *The Modern Theatre.* New York: The Macmillan Company, 1964.

HOGAN, ROBERT, and SVEN ERIC MOLIN. *Drama: The Major Genres.* New York: Dodd, Mead & Company, 1962.

REINERT, OTTO. *Drama: An Introductory Anthology.* Boston: Little, Brown and Company, 1961.

———. *Modern Drama*. Boston: Little, Brown and Com
pany, 1961.

B. Dramatic Theory and Criticism

BENTLEY, ERIC. *The Playwright As Thinker*. New York
William Morrow and Company, 1946; Meridian Book
1957.

BUTCHER, S. H. *Aristotle's Theory of Poetry and Fine Ar
New York: Dover Publications, Inc., 1951.

CLARK, BARRETT H. *European Theories of the Drama*. Rev
ed. New York: Crown Publishers, Inc., 1947.

COLE, TOBY (ed.). *Playwrights on Playwriting*. New York
Hill & Wang, 1960.

GASSNER, JOHN. *Masters of the Drama*. 3rd ed. New York
Dover Publications, Inc., 1954.

———. *Ideas in the Drama*. New York: Columbia Unive
sity Press, 1964.

HARTNOLL, PHYLLIS (ed.). *Oxford Companion to th
Theatre*. 2nd ed. rev. London: Oxford University Pres
1957.

KITTO, H. D. F. *Greek Tragedy*. Garden City, N. Y.
Doubleday & Company, Inc., 1955.

KRUTCH, JOSEPH WOOD. *"Modernism" in Modern Dram*
Ithaca, N. Y.: Cornell University Press, 1953.

McCOLLOM, WILLIAM C. *Tragedy*. New York: Macmilla
Company, 1957.

MEYERS, HENRY ALONZO. *Tragedy, A View of Life*. Ithac
N. Y.: Cornell University Press, 1956.

NICOLL, ALLARDYCE. *An Introduction to Dramatic Theor*
4th ed. rev. London: G. G. Harrap, 1958.

POTTS, L. J. *Comedy*. London: Hutchinson Universit
Library, 1949.

ROWE, KENNETH THORPE. *A Theatre in Your Head*. Ne
York: Funk & Wagnalls Company, 1960.

SEWALL, RICHARD BENSON. *The Vision of Tragedy.* New Haven, Conn.: Yale University Press, 1959.

SYPHER, WYLIE (ed.). *Comedy: An Essay on Comedy, by George Meredith. Laughter, by Henri Bergson. The Meaning of Comedy, by Wylie Sypher.* Garden City, N. Y.: Doubleday & Company, Inc., 1956.

THOMPSON, ALAN REYNOLDS. *The Anatomy of Drama.* 2nd ed. Berkeley, Calif.: University of California Press, 1948.

————. *The Dry Mock, a Study of Irony in Drama.* Berkeley, Calif.: University of California Press, 1948.

Index

A

Abbey Theatre, 66
Action, 25
AESCHYLUS, 5
Ah! Wilderness (O'Neill), 68
Anatomy of Drama, The (Thompson), 72
ANOUILH, JEAN, 12
Antagonist, 15
Antagonistic force, 15
Antigone, 12, 23
Antigone (Sophocles), 18, 65
Antirealism, 77
Antirealistic style, 77
Antony, Marc, 26
Arena staging, 77
ARISTOTLE, 2, 5, 14, 63, 70

B

BARRIE, J. M., 6
Blood Wedding (Lorca), 12
Bolingbroke, 26
Boor, The (Chekhov), 65, 68
Brutus, 26

C

Catastrophe, 17, 24
CHEKHOV, ANTON, 65, 68, 76
Climax, 17, 23
Comedy, 68
  high, 68
  light, 68
  of ideas, 69

Comedy (*Cont.*)
  of manners, 69
  neoclassical, 75
  realistic, 75
Comedy of Errors, 68
Comic vision, 69
Complication, 17, 23, 24
Confidant (confidante), 15
Conflict, 16, 17
Conventions, dramatic, 11

D

Denouement, 17, 23, 24
Desire Under the Elms (O'Neill), 76
Deus ex machina, 24
Dialogue, 25 ff.
Dramatic elements, 2
Dramatic present, 2
Drame, 69, 70

E

Ensemble acting, 76
Exposition, 17
Expressionism, 76
EURIPIDES, 5

F

Fantasy, 77
Farce, 65, 67
FEYDEAU, GEORGE, 68
Foil, 15
FRANCE, ANATOLE, 68

G

Ghosts (Ibsen), 72
Globe Theatre, 8
GORKY, MAXIM, 76

H

Hedda Gabler, 16
Henry V, 20
Hernani (Hugo), 66
HUGO, VICTOR, 16

I

IBSEN, HENRIK, 7, 8, 18, 72, 76
Importance of Being Earnest, The (Wilde), 68
Inciting force, 17, 23
INGE, WILLIAM, 15
Irony, 62
  dramatic, 62
  Sophoclean, 62

J

JAMES, HENRY, 6, 13
JONSON, BEN, 69
Juno and the Paycock (O'Casey), 76

K

Katharsis, 71
Keep an Eye on Amélie (Feydeau), 68

L

Lark, The (Anouilh), 12
Life with Father (Lindsay and Crouse), 68
LORCA, FEDERICO GARCIA, 12
Lower Depths, The (Gorky), 76

M

Man Who Married a Dumb Wife, The (France), 68
Mary, Queen of Scots, 12
MATTHEWS, BRANDER, 14
Melodrama, 69
MOLIERE, 15, 68, 69
Moscow Art Theatre, 76

N

NATHAN, GEORGE JEAN, 8
Naturalism, 75, 77

O

O'CASEY, SEAN, 66, 76
Oedipus of Thebes, 12
Oedipus the King (Sophocles), 65
O'NEILL, EUGENE, 68, 76

P

PINERO, SIR ARTHUR WING, 33
Plot, 14
  parts of, 16 ff.
Plough and the Stars, The (O'Casey), 66
Poetics (Aristotle), 5, 70
Presentational style, 76
Problem play, 62, 69, 70
Prologue, 19, 20
Proposal, The (Chekhov), 65, 68
Protagonist, 8, 15, 71
Purposive will, 17

R

RACINE, JEAN, 72
Realism, 76

Resolution, 17
RICE, ELMER, 76
Richard II, 12, 26
Rising action, 17, 23
Rivals, The (Sheridan), 20, 26
Romeo and Juliet, 8, 18, 19, 23

S

Saint Joan (Shaw), 12
Satire, 68
SAROYAN, WILLIAM, 15
Scapin (Molière), 68
School for Scandal, The (Sheridan), 20
Second Mrs. Tanqueray, The (Pinero), 30, 33
SHAKESPEARE, WILLIAM, 5, 6, 7, 15, 66, 67, 68
SHAW, GEORGE BERNARD, 6, 7, 12
SHERIDAN, RICHARD BRINSLEY, 20, 26
SOPHOCLES, 5, 7
Stage business, 26
STANISLAVSKY, KONSTANTIN, 76

Street Scene (Rice), 76
Symbolism, 76

T

Tartuffe (Molière), 69
Theater in the round, 77
Theater of the absurd, 78
Theatricalism, 76
Theme, 61 ff.
THOMPSON, ALAN REYNOLDS, 72
Tragedy, 70 ff.
    classical, 65
    neoclassical, 75
    romantic, 75
Turning point, 17, 24
Types of drama, 65 ff.

V

Volpone (Jonson), 69

W

What Every Woman Knows (Barrie), 6
WILDE, OSCAR, 68

Y

YEATS, W. B., 66